B. Chirva

FOOTBALL
Improving the goalkeepers play when caught wrong-footed and in two tempo

2014

УДК 796 332
Ч 64

Ч 64 **Chirva B.** Football. Improving the goalkeepers play when caught wrong-footed and in two tempo. – Moscow, 2014. – 136 с.

ISBN 978-5-98724-115-8

This monograph presents methods of perfection of catching and blocking the ball when caught wrong-footed and in two tempo by experienced goalkeepers.

The concept of goalkeepers' play when caught wrong-footed and in two tempo is given and specificity of their actions in these situations is considered. A set of exercises for training of catching and blocking the ball when caught wrong-footed and in two tempo by goalkeepers, developed from analysis of highly experienced goalkeepers' actions in games and patterns of successful performance of catching and blocking of moving objects.

УДК 796 332
Ч 64

ISBN 978-5-98724-184-4

CONTENTS

For notes

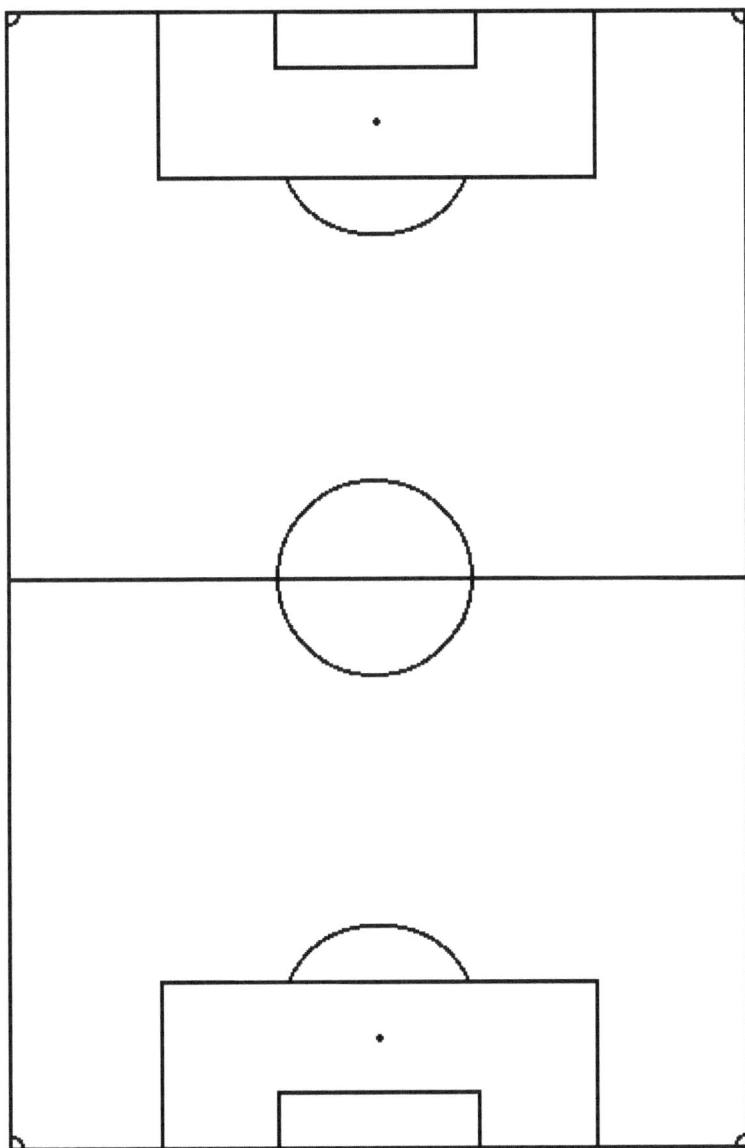

INTRODUCTION

Generally catching and blocking the ball by goalkeepers as such is the finishing of set of motive and psyhomotor actions. Depending on situation preparative actions before catching and blocking the ball and movements at catching and blocking directly may be performed by goalkeepers in different directions and with a various speed.

Experience has proven there are two kinds of structure of goalkeepers' complex actions while catching and blocking the ball, namely:

– when caught wrong-footed goalkeepers have to perform preparative movements before catching or blocking the ball and movements at catching and blocking directly at different directions;

– in two tempo when situation requires goalkeepers to perform the second in a row attempt to catch or block the ball without a delay, beginning it from the position they were after the first attempt to catch or block the ball.

Specificity of goalkeepers actions while catching and blocking the ball when caught wrong-footed and in two tempo is considered and main areas of work while perfecting these actions are suggested in this book.

Methods of training catching and blocking the ball when caught wrong-footed and in two tempo by experienced goalkeepers, developed from analysis of highly experienced goalkeepers' actions in games, is given.

Sets of special goalkeeping exercises for perfecting certain actions occurring in various situations while playing when caught wrong-footed and in two tempo, and examples of drills performed by in-field players and also suggesting the possibility of training catching and blocking the ball by goalkeepers when caught wrong-footed and in two tempo, are represented.

LEGEND KEYS

Legend keys presented in fig. 1 below are used in describing goalkeepers' and players' actions and suggested drills in this book.

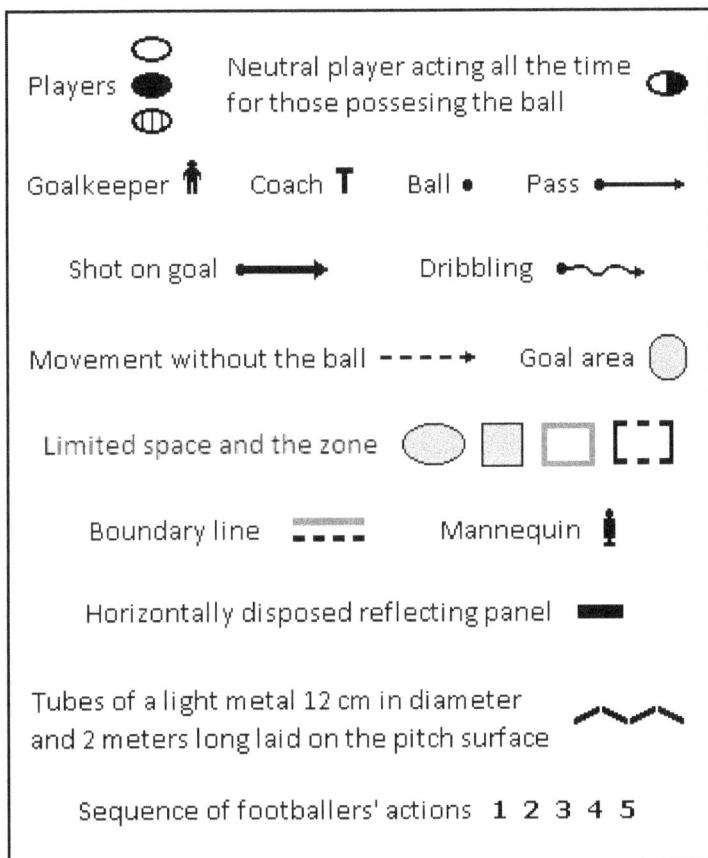

Fig. 1. Legend keys used in describing goalkeepers' and players' actions and suggested drills

For notes

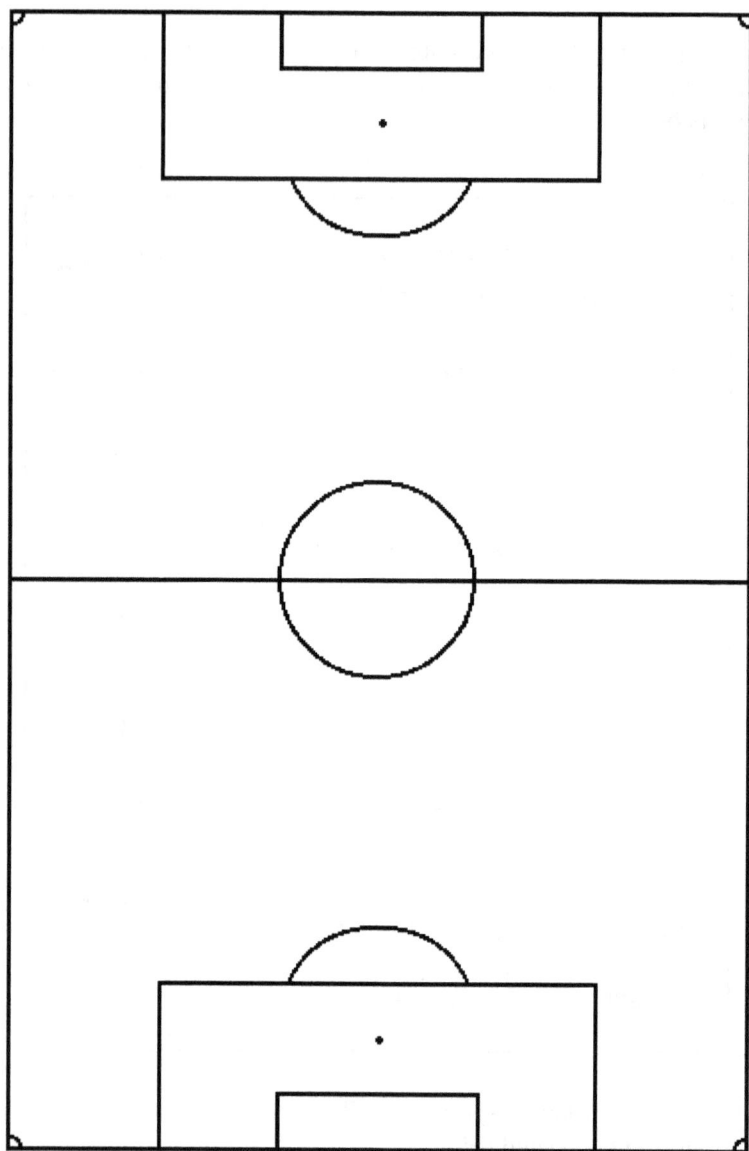

PART ONE
TRAINING CATCHING AND BLOCKING THE BALL WHEN CAUGHT WRONG-FOOTED

CHAPTER 1.
THE CONCEPT OF «GOALKEEPERS' PLAY WHEN CAUGHT WRONG-FOOTED»

In many game episodes goalkeepers have to begin the direct movement with the hand (hands) or leg to the ball for catching or blocking it in the course of moving performed by them to occupy the best position for catching or blocking the ball.

They often have to begin the direct movement with the hand (hands) or leg to the ball for catching or blocking it exactly in the course of moving. With that the direction of goalkeepers' movement up to the moment of sending the ball towards them and direction of their body and hands' movement to the ball for catching or blocking it may both coincide (for example, when the goalkeeper moves to the right and blocks the ball diving to the right) and not coincide and even be exactly opposite.

In some cases goalkeepers have to change the direction of their movements even during the ball's flight, as the trajectory of the ball's flight changes suddenly as a result of a bounce from players situated on its way.

Situations when goalkeepers must catch or block the ball, sent in direction opposite relative to the direction of their movement before the shot or which suddenly change the initial direction, may occur both while realization of various free kicks by the opponent and directly in the course of play (in open game). Success of goalkeepers' actions in these situations depends on abilities to play when caught wrong-footed.

Movements performed technically right form the basis of play when caught wrong-footed mastery, as they provide the speed of changing the direction of movement by goalkeepers and their direct movement to the ball for catching or blocking it.

Acting when caught wrong-footed, goalkeepers may apply various manners of catching and blocking the ball in supporting and non-supporting position.

All kinds of specific anticipation reactions occurring in their activities are important for successful goalkeepers' play, and exactly reactions of:

– anticipation of development of play situations and course of the game;

– anticipation of moment, speed and direction of sending the ball on shooting players' movements;

– anticipation of point and moment of coming into contact with the ball along its trajectory.

Concerning the anticipation of point and moment of coming into contact with the ball along its trajectory the meaning of goalkeepers' ability to change the direction of ocular movements while tracking the flight of the ball, determined by the speed of oculogyric and dynamic visual acuity, should be noted.

CHAPTER 2.
THE PROBLEM OF ORGANIZING OF TRAINING CATCHING AND BLOCKING THE BALL WHEN CAUGHT WRONG-FOOTED BY GOALKEEPERS

Overwhelmingly goalkeepers' attempts to catch and block the ball in games suggest actions when caught wrong-footed, and most of goals are conceded by goalkeepers in situations when they have to play when caught wrong-footed anyway.

With that, observations over trainings of youth and professional teams of different qualification show that most of drills for practicing shots on goal by players, occupying much of goalkeepers' training time, arranged so that goalkeepers have to catch and block the ball when caught wrong-footed not so often. This is due to the construction of drills and specificity of players' action while performing it.

Describing such exercises we can mark several characteristics.

First. In many exercises concluding with the shot on goal (both from within and outside of 18-yard box) players get keynote to shoot on goal from the specified area of the pitch (fig. 2).

Foreseeing from where should shot on goal be performed, goalkeepers can take specific position well ahead of its performance regardless of change of the ball position along the length and across the width of the pitch before the moment of sending it into the net.

Second. Even in exercises where the attack may be finished with shot on goal from one or another area by one of two-three players, not always goalkeepers have to catch and block the ball when caught wrong-footed while moving aside.

This is due to the specificity of players' actions while performing such drills.

14

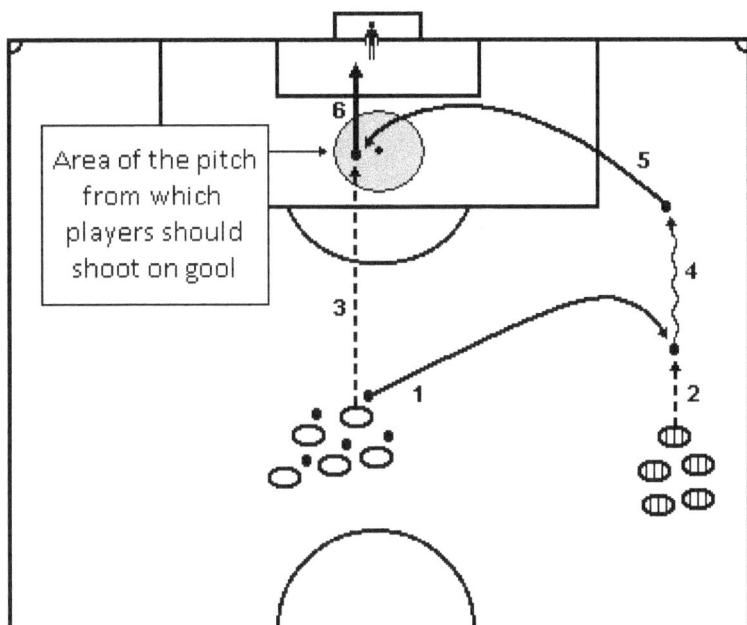

Fig. 2. Example of exercise for practicing shots on goal by players, along which the goalkeepers may take necessary position well ahead of sending the ball into the net for catching or blocking it, as players should perform shots on goal from the specified area of the pitch

Before shooting in goal players may pass the ball to each other across the width of the pitch, sending it with a lower speed on a long distance, and their partner who has to perform a finishing shot, may get to the shooting position in advance. Therefore goalkeepers have enough time to take necessary position for catching and blocking the ball in advance before the moment of shooting on goal.

Third. In certain (and in some cases in the most) part of drills finishing with a shot on goal, it is suggested to be performed by players from outside of the 18-yard box.

Though the father away from the goal-line protected by the goalkeepers the change of the ball position across the width of the pitch happens:

– the shorter in distance and time are movements of goalkeepers to the side for taking the necessary position for catching or blocking the ball;

– the more possibilities goalkeepers have to take such position some time before the sending the ball into the net.

Fourth. While shooting on goal players are usually not situated in space between the goalkeeper and the shooting point, and eventually there are no sudden changes in direction of the ball's flight as a result of touching it by players.

Fifth. If a drill is one or another variation of football with sufficiently high number of players in each team played in a considerable playing space, let alone game in full numbers on the pitch of standard size, then cases of goalkeepers' actions when caught wrong-footed are not numerous since the specificity of football itself.

As for special goalkeepers drills, tasks on practicing catching and blocking the ball when caught wrong-footed generally performed by goalkeepers to the extent deficient for growth of their skill in this aspect of play, and with that certain components of play when caught wrong-footed are often left out of account.

In connection with the above matter it seems necessary to emphasize on improving all actions when caught wrong-footed, occurring in matches, by goalkeepers in their training activities. With that the particular training of certain elements of play when caught wrong-footed by goalkeepers using specially organized goalkeeper drills gets emphasis.

CHAPTER 3.
SPECIFICITY OF GOALKEEPERS'
ACTIONS WHILE CATCHING
AND BLOCKING THE BALL
WHEN CAUGHT WRONG-FOOTED
IN VARIOUS SITUATIONS

Analysis of actions of high class goalkeepers has shown that their attempts to catch and block the ball when caught wrong-footed are performed in following typical play situations:

– when they move in one or another direction to take position for catching and blocking the ball before the moment when it is sent towards the goal;

– when the ball suddenly changes the trajectory during its flight as a result of a touch by the player situated between the goal and the shooting point.

3. 1. Situations when goalkeepers move to take position for catching and blocking the ball before it is sent towards the goal

All situations in which goalkeepers move to take position for catching and blocking the ball before it is sent towards the goal may be divided into two types from the point of view of ball position directly before it is sent towards the goal:

– the ball is in motion (while players' movements with the ball and passes on course of play);

– the ball is motionless (while penalty kicks, corners, free kicks).

In these situations goalkeepers may catch and block the ball when caught wrong-footed moving in different directions: to the side, forward, backward.

Goalkeepers' attempts to catch and block the ball when caught wrong-footed while moving to the side occur when:

– before the shot on goal player moves with the ball across the width of the pitch towards the 18-yard box or not far from it (fig. 3);

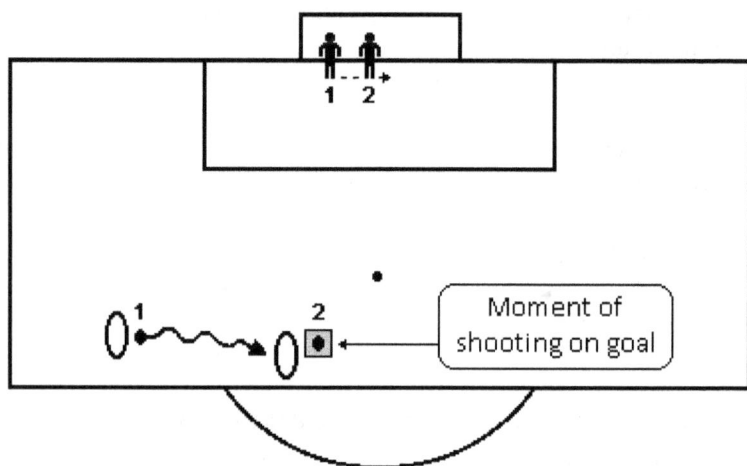

Fig. 3. Situation when before the shot on goal player moves with the ball across the width of the pitch and the goalkeeper moves to the side before the shooting moment

– a pass across the width of the pitch in the 18-yard box or not far from it on course of play or during free-kicks is performed before the shot on goal (fig. 4);

– penalty kick or free kick with sending the ball into the net is performed, while goalkeepers begin to move to the certain point of the goal before the shot, expecting to catch or block the ball there (fig. 5).

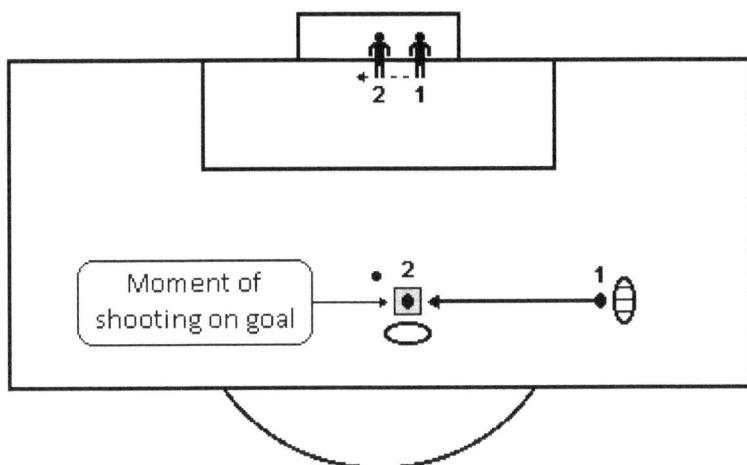

Fig. 4. Situation when before the shot on goal the ball is passed across the width of the pitch and the goalkeeper moves to the side before the shooting moment

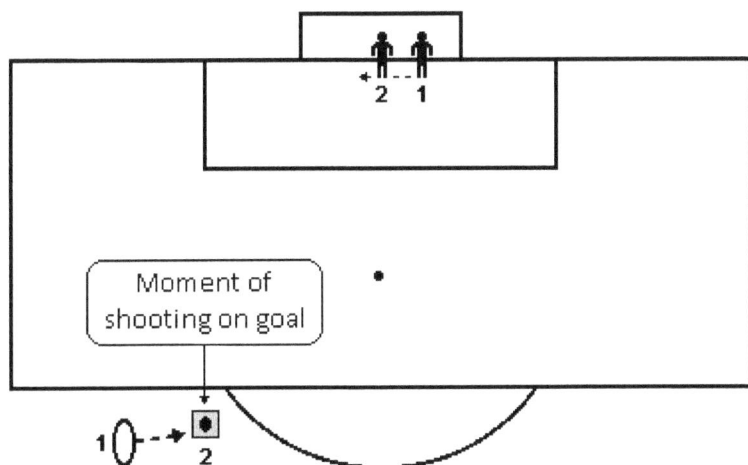

Fig. 5. Situation when shot on goal is performed from the free-kick and the goalkeeper moves to the side before the shooting moment

Catching and blocking the ball by goalkeepers when caught wrong-footed while moving backwards may be performed when goalkeepers get back to the goal after going forward, while player sends the ball across the width or along the length of the pitch into the area near the goal in front of the goalkeeper at that moment (fig. 6).

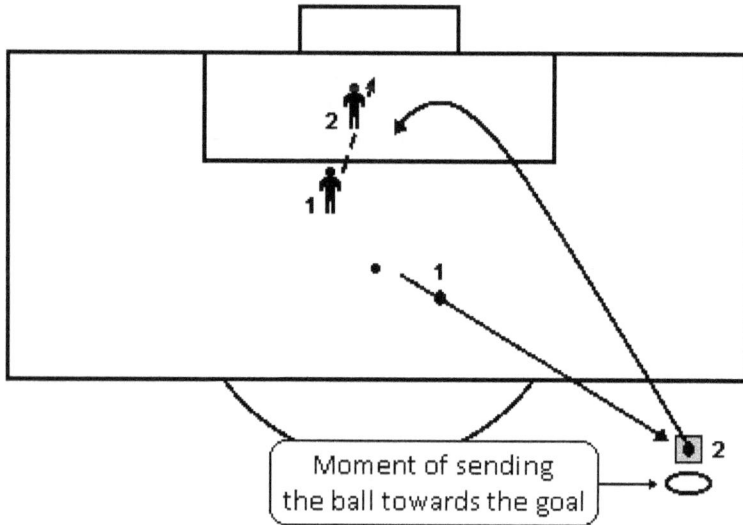

Fig. 6. Situations when goalkeeper moves to the goal after going forward, while player sends the ball into the area near the goal in front of the goalkeeper at that moment

It may become necessary for goalkeepers to catch and block the ball when caught wrong-footed while moving forward when:

– a pass across the width or along the length of the pitch into the 18-yard box on course of play or from free-kicks is performed before the shot on goal, and goalkeeper goes forward to catch or block the ball after a pass, but doesn't reach it having defined the meeting point incorrectly or as a result of obstacles from players (fig. 7);

Fig. 7. Situation when before the shot on goal the ball is passed across the width of the pitch and goalkeeper moves forward before the moment of shot for catching or blocking the ball after a pass, but doesn't get to it in time

– a pass across the width or along the length of the pitch is performed into the 18-yard box on course of play or from free-kicks, and goalkeeper goes forward to catch or block the ball after a pass, but drops the ball while catching or knocks it so that an opponent gets the opportunity to shoot on goal immediately (fig. 8).

While moving before the moment of sending the ball towards the goal, goalkeepers generally try to move fast, trying to finish moving and take position «major goalkeeper stance» in necessary position up to this moment. Though possible change in play situation may require them to stop quickly or change the direction of movement at any moment.

As practice shows, these two problems are more effectively solved by goalkeepers who move with sidesteps with correct techniques.

It also has to be noticed that in football nowadays great bulk of goals (around 80%) is scored with a first touch with leg and head on course of play.

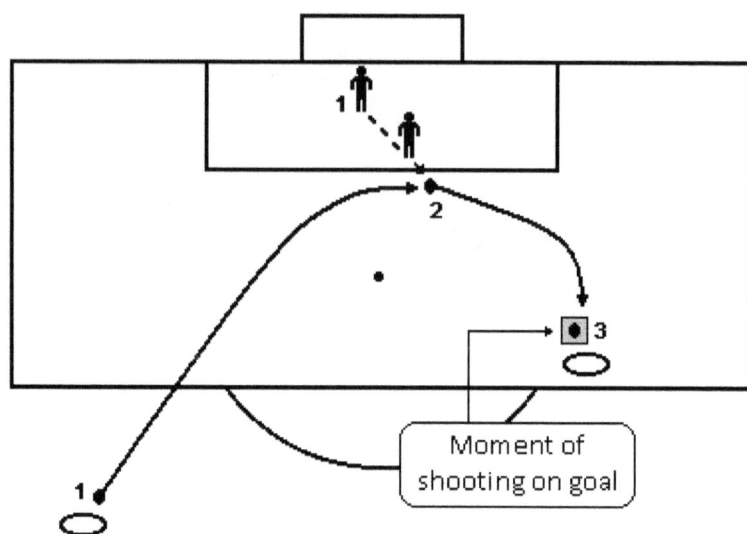

Fig. 8. Situation where the ball is sent into the 18-yard box and the goalkeeper moves forwards for catching or blocking the ball after a pass, but knocks it so that the opponent can shoot on goal immediately

This means that definite part of goals is conceded by goalkeepers in situations when the ball quickly changes its position by several meters across the width of the pitch before it is sent into the net with a first touch.

In these cases success of catching and blocking the ball when caught wrong-footed depends on goalkeepers' ability to switch from one variant of tracing the ball to another quickly, exactly from tracing the ball moving in front of them from the right to left or from the left to the right to tracing the ball flying towards them.

3. 2. Situations the ball flying towards the goal suddenly changes its trajectory as a result of a player's touch

Not so often, but there are situations in goalkeepers' play when they have already begun to perform actions for catching or blocking the ball sent towards the goal, whereas the ball suddenly changes it trajectory as a result of a touch by the player (partner, opponent) who is situated in the ball's way on one or another distance from the goal (fig. 9).

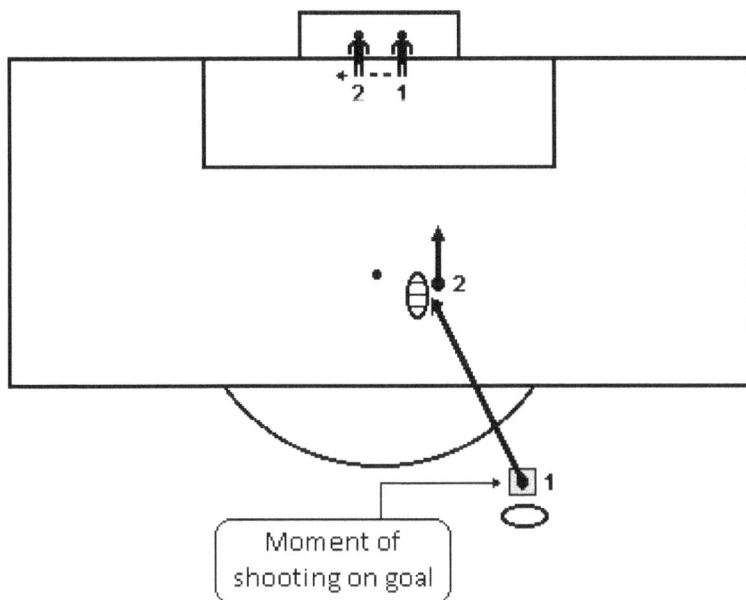

Fig. 9. Situation when the goalkeeper begins to move to the side for catching or blocking the ball flying into the net, whereas the ball suddenly changed the trajectory of flight towards the goal as a result of a touch by the player

Such situations may occur while sending the ball towards the goal both with a foot kick (on course of play and from free-kicks) and a head kick. The more players concentrated in the area in front of the goal, the higher the probability of the ball rebounding off the player.

There are three new possible trajectories towards the goal after the ball's collision with the player on its way:
– across the pitch surface;
– with a rebound off the pitch surface;
– on air at different heights.

Change in initial direction of the ball's flight towards the goal as a result of a touch by the player may happen on different stages of performing of preparative and direct actions for catching and blocking the ball by the goalkeeper.

In this regard the success of catching and blocking the ball by goalkeepers when caught wrong-footed while bouncing off the player depends on quickness of:
– switching from tracing the trajectory of the ball in initial direction to tracing its trajectory in new direction (speed of oculogyric);
– transition from performing of actions in one direction (at a certain stage) to another (speed of body shifting).

Besides of that, efficiency of goalkeepers' actions in these cases largely depends on such factor as psychic determination to perform the second in a row move to the ball for catching or blocking it, which they often have to begin from uncomfortable position, even from lying position.

CHAPTER 4.
MAIN STRANDS OF WORK
WHILE TRAINING CATCHING
AND BLOCKING THE BALL
BY GOALKEEPERS WHEN
CAUGHT WRONG-FOOTED

Perfection of catching and blocking the ball by goalkeepers when caught wrong-footed suggests two main strands of work:

– training of certain actions occurring while playing when caught wrong-footed in different situations using specially organized goalkeeper drills;

– training of play when caught wrong-footed in whole in the context of those team exercises in which situations of catching and blocking the ball when caught wrong-footed in games may be simulated.

It should be noted that labeling of goalkeepers' actions such as «catching and blocking the ball when caught wrong-footed» points at importance of technically proper performance of these movements by them in these cases. In this regard while performing both types of exercises goalkeepers should pay particular attention to technique of moving with sidesteps, which suggests it's necessary to:

1. Not to take too wide and too narrow steps.

2. No to cross leg.

3. Not to lose contact with the pitch by two legs simultaneously, for what, having stepped by one leg, to pull the another to it just after the former stands on the pitch.

4. Moving with bent legs and body and head slightly leaning forward, so it is possible to involve flexible component of leg muscles while repulsion off the pitch.

5. To try to equipoise the body avoiding its significant wavering.

CHAPTER 5.
SPECIAL EXERCISES FOR
TRAINING CATCHING
AND BLOCKING THE BALL
BY GOALKEEPERS WHEN
CAUGHT WRONG-FOOTED
IN VARIOUS SITUATIONS

5. 1. Organizing special exercises for training of catching and blocking the ball by goalkeepers when caught wrong-footed

Taking into account the specificity of goalkeepers' actions while catching and blocking the ball when caught wrong-footed in games, developed are two sets of special goalkeeper exercises for training of playing when caught wrong-footed in situations when:
– goalkeepers move in one or another direction to take position for catching or blocking the ball before the moment when it is sent towards the goal;
– on course of flight towards the goal the ball suddenly changes its trajectory as a result of a touch by the player situated on its way.

Exercises for training of catching and blocking the ball when caught wrong-footed in situations when goalkeepers move before the moment of sending the ball towards the goal suggest practicing these actions while moving to the side, forward and backward.

Special conditions are set in some of these exercises to improve quality of performing certain specific for playing when caught wrong-footed technical elements and bunches of actions (movements, techniques of catching and blocking the ball) by goalkeepers, while in other the problem of perfection of catching and blocking the ball when caught wrong-footed by goalkeepers is solved in whole.

As for the organization of exercises for training catching and blocking the ball when caught wrong-footed by goalkeepers in situation when on course of flight the ball suddenly changes its trajectory as a result of a touch by the player, there are some definite complications.

Firstly it is due to the fact, that in matches bounces off a player into the net are unpredictable and occasional, so the intentional simulation of fully natural situation of the ball ricochet into the net during the training is problematic as such.

There may be marked several fundamentals that should be noticed while constructing exercises for perfection of catching and blocking the ball when caught wrong-footed by goalkeepers, when on course of flight the ball suddenly changes its trajectory as a result of a touch by the player.

First. In these exercises should be set such conditions that at first goalkeeper necessarily begins to perform real actions for catching or blocking the flying ball in one direction, but then at some point is forced to readjust for performing actions for catching and blocking the ball in another direction.

Such conditions may be provided including using in specific task repeat two balls sent consequently in different relative to the goalkeeper directions.

Second. For training of catching and blocking the ball when caught wrong-footed by goalkeepers it is also important that after a bounce off the player on its way or after ricochet simulation balls fly not just in new direction relative to the goalkeepers, but at trajectories of definite range, at a definite distance from the goalkeeper and in definite speed range.

Necessary speed of the ball after a ricochet and precision of its hitting the necessary area can be achieved with throws of smaller balls (tennis or handball) by hand.

Third. The greatest improvements in play when caught wrong-footed mastery may be achieved providing that during exercises they:

– perform relatively high number of attempts of catching and blocking the ball suddenly changing its trajectory on course of flight towards the goal;

– alternate attempts of catching and blocking and catching the ball suddenly changing its trajectory on course of flight towards the goal with attempts of catching and blocking the ball which trajectory doesn't change after sending towards the goal at random.

Observance of these two conditions of gaining maximum training effect requires not only the certain construction of drills, but also the increasing of baseline minimum time of performance.

Developed set of drills for training catching and blocking the ball when caught wrong-footed by goalkeepers in situations when on course of its flight towards the goal the ball bouncing off the player includes tasks for perfection of these actions while the ball is moving in the new direction:

– across the pitch surface;

– with a rebound off the pitch surface;

– at different heights above the pitch surface.

Various mechanical facilities (reflecting panels placed at different angles) are used in some part of these exercises for changing trajectory of the ball in the required direction and then its flight at the required trajectory.

Following are sets of special exercises for training catching and blocking the ball when caught wrong-footed by goalkeepers in situations when:

– they move in one or another direction to take position for catching or blocking the ball before the moment when it is sent towards the goal;

– the ball flying towards the goal suddenly changes its trajectory as a result of a touch by the player situated on its way.

5. 2. A set of special exercises for training catching and blocking the ball when caught wrong-footed by goalkeepers in case of movement before the moment of sending the ball towards the goal

Drills for training the technique of movement with quick change of direction to opposite

Drill 1	
Drill description	**Technical tips**
The goalkeeper is positioned in «major goalkeeper stance» outside the goal, the coach – opposite to the goalkeeper few meters from him. The coach shows the goalkeepers the direction, speed and duration of movement to the left, to the right, forward and backward with successive low-amplitude motions with a hand raised so that the last: – moves in specified direction at a distance from 2-3 to 5-6 steps; – changes the direction of movement without strict sequence and delay; – performs various number of steps in different direction. The goalkeeper moves **with sidesteps** trying to respond to changing of motion parameters by the coach at a maximum speed. In one repeat the coach demand from the goalkeeper to change the direction of movement 4-6 times. Varying the speed of a hand motion, the coach may demand from the goalkeeper to move in different directions faster of slower	– the goalkeeper should move with sidesteps with bent legs without stepping too broadly or narrowly; – the goalkeeper should not lose contact with the pitch by two legs simultaneously, for what, having stepped by one leg, to pull the another to it just after the former stands on the pitch; – goalkeeper should try to change the direction of movement to the opposite as quick as possible

Drill 2	
Drill description	**Technical tips**
Quick transition from normal running to the side, forward and backward to moving with sidesteps in the opposite direction **Variant 1. Movement to the side** The goalkeeper is positioned in «major goalkeeper stance» outside of the goal with a right (fig. 1A) or left (fig. 1B) flank to two parallel lines 3 meters long marked at 3 and 6 meters from him. **Fig. 1** On signal the goalkeeper begins to move quickly to the right or left side with normal running half-sideways towards up to the line marked at 6 meters from him, then abruptly changes the direction of movement and begins to move back quickly with sidesteps with a left (fig. 2A) or right (fig. 2B) flank subsequently towards up to the line marked at 3 meters from his initial position **Fig. 2**	– goalkeeper should move with normal running quickly; – goalkeeper should try to change the direction of movement to opposite as quick as possible; – while moving with sidesteps goalkeeper should be with bent legs without stepping too broadly or narrowly; – while moving with sidesteps the goalkeeper should not lose contact with the pitch by two legs simultaneously, for what, having stepped by one leg, to pull the another to it just after the former stands on the pitch; – while moving both with normal running and sidesteps goalkeeper should orientate his head perpendicularly to the direction of movement

30

Drill 2 continuation

Variant 2. Moving back and forth and vice-versa

The goalkeeper is positioned in «major goalkeeper stance» outside of the goal face (fig. 1A) or back (fig. 1B) to two parallel lines 3 meters long marked at 3 and 6 meters from him.

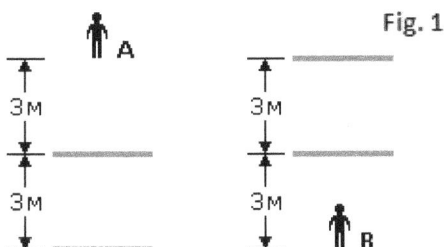

Fig. 1

On signal the goalkeeper begins to move quickly frontwise or back forward with **normal running** up to the line marked at 6 meters from him, then abruptly changes the direction of movement and begins to move back quickly **with sidesteps** back forward (fig. 2A) or frontwise (fig. 2B) subsequently towards up to the line marked at 3 meters from his initial position

Fig. 2

1 - frontwise
2 - back forward

– goalkeeper should move with normal running quickly;
– goalkeeper should try to change the direction of movement to opposite as quick as possible;
– while moving with sidesteps goalkeeper should be with bent legs without stepping too broadly or narrowly;
– while moving with sidesteps the goalkeeper should not lose contact with the pitch by two legs simultaneously, for what, having stepped by one leg, to pull the another to it just after the former stands on the pitch;
– while moving both with normal running and sidesteps goalkeeper should orientate his head in the direction same with the initial position

Drill 3	
Drill description	**Technical tips**
Taking the specific position by the goalkeeper while moving to the side, forward and back depending on the ball's position **Variant 1. Taking the specific position while changing the ball's location across the width of the pitch** A limited space 6 meters wide and 1.5 meters long is marked, divided into three zones: the middle 3 meters wide, the right and the left 1,5 meters wide each. The goalkeeper is positioned in «major goalkeeper stance» in the middle zone, three goalkeeper's partners – in range in front of the goalkeeper 5 meters from him and 5 meters from each other, the partner opposite to the goalkeeper has the ball in his hands (fig. 1). Goalkeeper's partners begin to pass the ball quickly to each other with hands with mounted trajectory and with a rebound off the pitch surface chaotically providing that in one repeat may be performed: – no more than four passes overall; – only one direct pass between the goalkeeper's partners positioned 10 meters from each other.	– the goalkeeper's partners have to pass the ball to each other without a delay, effectively forcing the goalkeeper to move quickly and change the direction of movement to the opposite; – the goalkeeper should move with sidesteps with bent legs without stepping too broadly or narrowly; – the goalkeeper should not lose contact with the pitch by two legs simultaneously, for what, having stepped by one leg, to pull the another to it just after the former stands on the pitch; – the goalkeeper's partners have to try to finish each task repeat surprisingly for the goalkeeper, hitting the pitch surface with the ball at a maximum speed

Fig. 1

Drill 3 continuation

The goalkeeper quickly moves **with sidesteps** in limited space to the left or to the right so that at the time on reception of the ball by one of partners to be both legs:
– in the middle zone if the ball is received by the partner positioned opposite to the goalkeeper;
– in the right or in the left zone if the ball is received by the partner positioned to the right or to left of the goalkeeper.
After any pass the goalkeeper's partner who has received the ball may hit the pitch surface with it. If the goalkeeper is both legs in proper zone, he wins in this repeat of the task (fig. 2A). Otherwise, the goalkeeper's partners win (fig. 2B).

Fig. 2

A

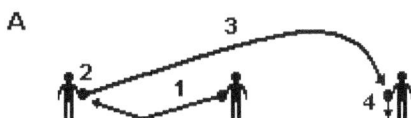

B

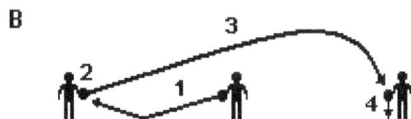

Drill 3 continuation

Variant 2 Taking the specific position while changing the ball's location along the length of the pitch

A limited space 1,5 meters wide and 6 meters long is marked, divided into three zones: the middle 3 meters long, the front and the back 1,5 meters long each.

The goalkeeper is positioned in «major goalkeeper stance» in the middle zone, three goalkeeper's partners – in column in front of the goalkeeper 5 meters from each other: the closest 4 meters from the goalkeeper, the middle – with the ball in hands (fig. 3).

Fig. 3

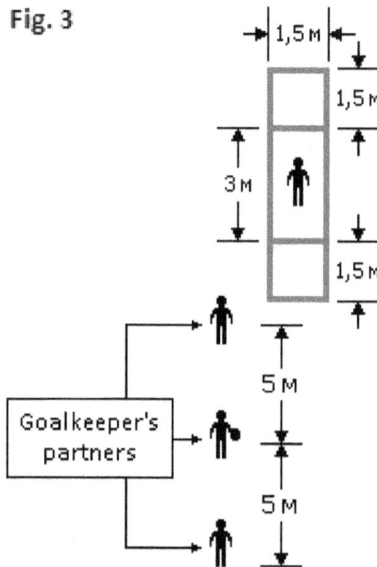

Goalkeeper's partners begin to pass the ball quickly to each other with hands with mounted trajectory and with a rebound off the pitch surface chaotically providing that in one repeat may be performed:

– the goalkeeper's partners have to pass the ball to each other without a delay, effectively forcing the goalkeeper to move quickly and change the direction of movement to the opposite;

– the goalkeeper should move with sidesteps with bent legs without stepping too broadly or narrowly;

– the goalkeeper should not lose contact with the pitch by two legs simultaneously, for what, having stepped by one leg, to pull the another to it just after the former stands on the pitch;

– the goalkeeper's partners have to try to finish each task repeat surprisingly for the goalkeeper, hitting the pitch surface with the ball at a maximum speed

Drill 3 continuation

– no more than four passes overall;
– only one direct pass between the goalkeeper's partners positioned 10 meters from each other.

The goalkeeper quickly moves **with sidesteps** in limited space forward or backward so that at the time on reception of the ball by one of partners to be both legs:

– in the middle zone if the ball is received by the middle partner;

– in the front or back zone if the ball is received by the distant or closest partner.

After any pass the goalkeeper's partner who has received the ball may hit the pitch surface with it. If the goalkeeper is both legs in proper zone, he wins in this repeat of the task (fig. 4A). Otherwise, the goalkeeper's partners win (fig. 4B)

Fig. 4

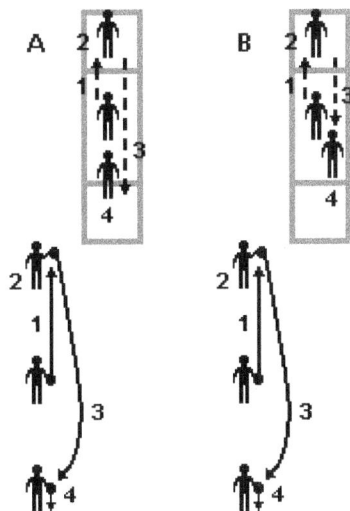

Drill 4	
Drill description	**Technical tips**
Catching the ball sent with hands when caught wrong-footed after moving to the side, forward and backward **Variant 1. Catching the ball after moving to the side** The goalkeeper is positioned in «major goalkeeper stance» outside the goal, the coach with the ball – opposite to the goalkeeper 5 meters from him. The goalkeeper begins to move **with sidesteps** to the left or to the right. As soon as the goalkeeper makes 3-4 steps, the coach sends the ball with a hand towards the point of his initial position with different trajectories (across the pitch surface, with a rebound off the pitch surface and with a mounted trajectory) so that he could catch the ball when caught wrong-footed in supporting position, while diving and jumping. The goalkeeper catches the ball when caught wrong-footed, sends it back to the coach and takes the initial position. Number of passes to the goalkeeper is 3-4 during his movement in every direction with different trajectories of the ball	– the goalkeeper should move with sidesteps with bent legs without stepping too broadly or narrowly; – the goalkeeper should not lose contact with the pitch by two legs simultaneously, for what, having stepped by one leg, to pull the another to it just after the former stands on the pitch; – the coach should send the ball towards the point of the goalkeeper's initial position timely and precisely, providing him with conditions for catching the ball when caught wrong-footed; – the goalkeeper should switch quickly from moving to the left or to the right to catching the ball the caught wrong-footed in supporting position, while diving and jumping

Drill 4 continuation

Variant 2. Catching the ball after moving forward and backward	– the goalkeeper

Variant 2. Catching the ball after moving forward and backward
The goalkeeper is positioned in «major goalkeeper stance» outside the goal, the coach with the ball – opposite to the goalkeeper 5 meters from him.

The goalkeeper begins to move **with sidesteps** forward of backward.

As soon as the goalkeeper makes 3-4 steps, the coach sends the ball with a hand towards the point of his initial position with different trajectories (across the pitch surface, with a rebound off the pitch surface and with a mounted trajectory) so that he could catch the ball when caught wrong-footed in supporting position, while diving and jumping.

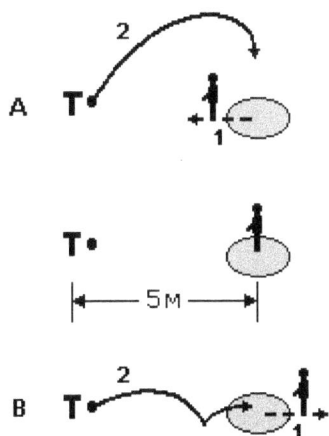

The goalkeeper catches the ball when caught wrong-footed, sends it back to the coach and takes the initial position.

Number of passes to the goalkeeper is 3-4 during his movement in every direction with different trajectories of the ball

– the goalkeeper should move with sidesteps with bent legs without stepping too broadly or narrowly;

– the goalkeeper should not lose contact with the pitch by two legs simultaneously, for what, having stepped by one leg, to pull the another to it just after the former stands on the pitch;

– the coach should send the ball towards the point of the goalkeeper's initial position timely and precisely, providing him with conditions for catching the ball when caught wrong-footed;

– the goalkeeper should switch quickly from moving to the left or to the right to catching the ball the caught wrong-footed in supporting position, while diving and jumping

Drills for training catching and blocking the ball when caught wrong-footed while moving to the side

Drill 1	
Drill description	**Technical tips**
The goalkeepers is positioned in the middle of the goal, the coach with the ball – opposite to one of the goal posts 10 meters from the goal-line (fig. 1). **Fig. 1** The goalkeeper begins to move towards the post the coach is opposite to, for taking the proper position for catching or blocking the ball in case the coach shoots on goal. After the goalkeeper made two-three steps the coach sends the ball with the leg into the net **necessarily** opposite to the goalkeeper's movement to the side from him at a distance of actual reach with different trajectories with a medium speed.	– the goalkeeper should move with sidesteps with bent legs without stepping too broadly or narrowly; – the goalkeeper should not lose contact with the pitch by two legs simultaneously, for what, having stepped by one leg, to pull the another to it just after the former stands on the pitch; – the goalkeeper has to be ready for possible sending the ball opposite to his movement to the moment when the coach shoots on goal; – the coach should send the ball opposite to the goalkeeper's movement timely and precisely so that catching or blocking the ball when caught wrong-footed were enforceable;

Drill 1 continuation

The goalkeeper catches or blocks the ball when caught wrong-footed (fig. 2).

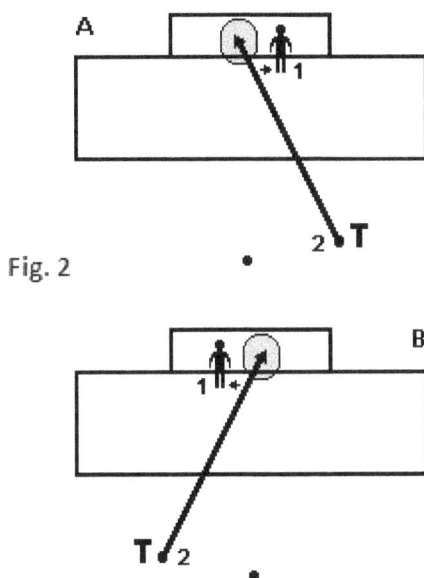

A

Fig. 2

2 T

B

T 2

Variant: the coach sends the ball **chaotically** in different repeats in the goal area where the goalkeeper initially moves to and opposite to his movement (fig. 3)

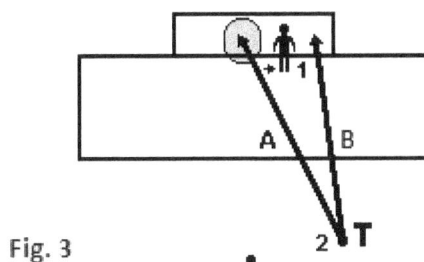

A   B

Fig. 3

2 T

– in certain repeats the coach should send the ball into the net with a rebound off the pitch surface, for what perform shots on goal from hands with foot;
– the goalkeeper should switch quickly from moving to the side to catching or blocking the ball when caught wrong-footed;
– the goalkeeper may catch or block the ball when caught wrong-footed in supporting position, while diving and jumping depending in direction and speed of sending the ball by the coach

Drill 2	
Drill description	**Technical tips**
The goalkeeper's partner with the ball is positioned opposite to the goal area angle 10 meters from the goal-line, the goalkeeper – in the goal for catching and blocking the ball in case his partner shoots the ball into the net (fig. 1).	– the goalkeeper should move with sidesteps with bent legs without stepping too broadly or narrowly;
Fig. 1	– the goalkeeper should not lose contact with the pitch by two legs simultaneously, for what, having stepped by one leg, to pull the another to it just after the former stands on the pitch; – the goalkeeper has to be ready for possible sending the ball opposite to his movement to the moment when the partner shoots on goal;
The goalkeeper's partner begins to move with the ball towards the penalty spot. The goalkeeper moves to the side, taking the proper position for catching or blocking the ball tacking into the account the change in its position. After moving a few meters the goalkeeper's partner sends the ball with the leg into the net **necessarily** opposite to the goalkeeper's movement to the side from him at a distance of actual reach with different trajectories with a medium speed.	– the goalkeeper's partner should send the ball surprisingly for the goalkeeper opposite to his movement, for what perform a shot on goal in different repeats after moving with the ball at a distance from 4 to 8 meters;

Drill 2 continuation

The goalkeeper catches or blocks the ball when caught wrong-footed (fig. 2).

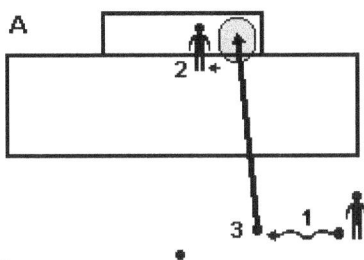

A

Fig. 2

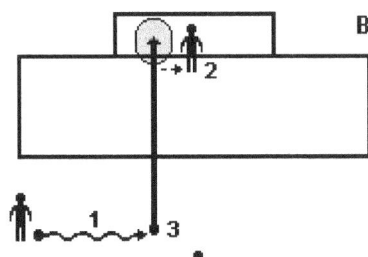

B

Variant: the goalkeeper's partner sends the ball **chaotically** in different repeats in the goal area on the goalkeeper's initial way of movement and opposite to his movement (fig. 3)

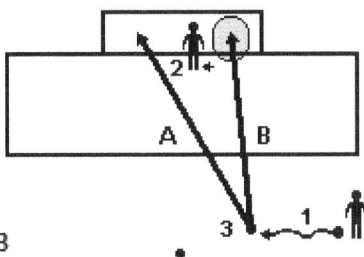

A   **B**

Fig. 3

– the goalkeeper's partner should vary the speed of moving with the ball in different repeats, forcing the goalkeeper to move faster of slower for taking the proper position for catching or blocking the ball;
– the goalkeeper's partner should send the ball opposite to the goalkeeper's movement precisely so that catching or blocking the ball when caught wrong-footed were enforceable;
– the goalkeeper should switch quickly from moving to the side to catching or blocking the ball when caught wrong-footed;
– the goalkeeper may catch or block the ball when caught wrong-footed in supporting position, while diving and jumping depending in direction and speed of sending the ball by the partner

Drill 3	
Drill description	**Technical tips**
The goalkeeper is positioned in the middle of the goal, the coach and two partners – in range in front of the goalkeeper 5 meters from each other and 10 meters from the goal-line, the coach with the ball – opposite to the middle of the goal (fig. 1). 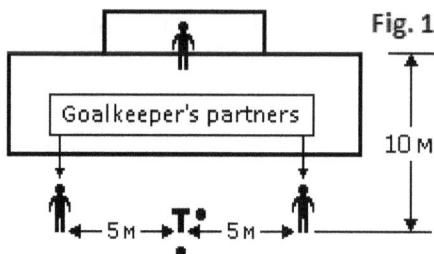 **Fig. 1** The coach sends the ball with a foot to one of the goalkeeper's partners. The goalkeeper moves to the side for taking the proper position for catching or blocking the ball tacking into the account the change in its position. The goalkeeper's partner sends the ball with a first touch **chaotically** in different repeats in the goal area on the goalkeeper's initial way of movement and opposite to his movement with different trajectories. The goalkeeper catches or blocks the ball (fig. 2). 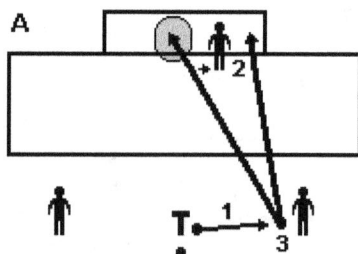 **Fig. 2**	– the coach should send the ball to one of the goalkeeper's partners surprisingly for the goalkeeper; – the goalkeeper should move with sidesteps with bent legs without stepping too broadly or narrowly; – the goalkeeper should not lose contact with the pitch by two legs simultaneously, for what, having stepped by one leg, to pull the another to it just after the former stands on the pitch; – the goalkeeper has to be ready for possible sending the ball opposite to his movement to the moment when the partner shoots on goal; – the goalkeeper should switch quickly from moving to the side to catching or blocking the ball when caught wrong-footed;

Drill 3 continuation

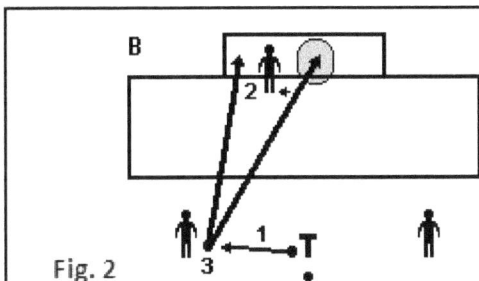

Fig. 2

Variant: in certain task repeats the goalkeeper's partner who has received the ball from the coach instead of shooting on goal pass the ball to the second partner, who sends it with a first touch in the goal area on the goalkeeper's initial way of movement and opposite to his movement with different trajectories (fig. 3)

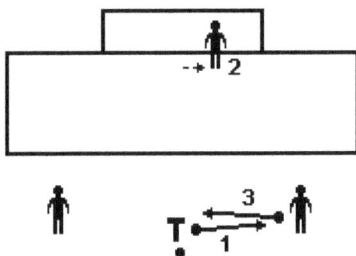

Fig. 3

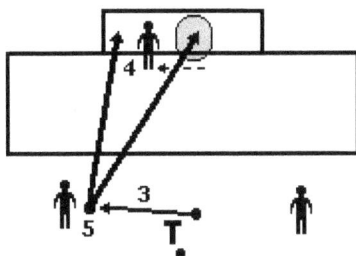

– the goalkeeper's partner who has received the ball from the coach and decided to pass the ball to the second partner instead of shooting on goal in one of task repeats should try to perform a pass with a first touch, surprisingly for the goalkeeper and comfortably for the partner to perform a shot on goal with a first touch;

– while the goalkeeper's partner perform a pass to the second partner instead of shooting on goal, the goalkeeper should again move to the side quickly to take the proper position for catching or blocking the ball tacking into the account the change in its position

Drill 4	
Drill description	**Technical tips**
The goalkeeper is positioned in the middle of the goal, three goalkeeper's partners – in range in front of the goalkeeper 5 meters from each other and 7 meters from the goal-line. The partner opposite to the goalkeeper has the ball in his hands (fig. 1). **Fig. 1** 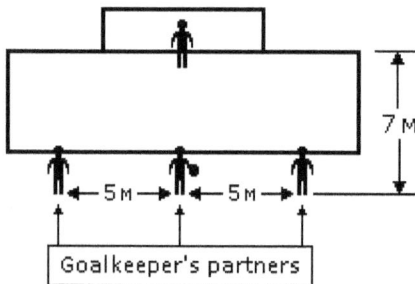 Goalkeeper's partners The goalkeeper's partners begin to pass the ball quickly to each other with hands with a mounted trajectory and with a high rebound off the pitch surface chaotically so that after every pass partner was comfortable to perform a header in the supporting position or while jumping. The goalkeeper moves to the side for taking the proper position for catching or blocking the ball tacking into the account the change in its position. After performing from one to three passes to each other by the goalkeeper's partners in different task repeats **chaotically** one of the them sends the ball with a head in the goal area on the goalkeeper's way to one or another direction or opposite to his movement: – with a mounted trajectory; – with a rebound off the pitch surface.	– the goalkeeper's partners have to pass the ball to each other without a delay, effectively forcing the goalkeeper to move quickly and change the direction of movement to the opposite; – the goalkeeper's partners may use dummies by showing the goalkeeper the direction of a pass to one partner while sending it to another; – the goalkeeper should move with sidesteps with bent legs without stepping too broadly or narrowly; – the goalkeeper should not lose contact with the pitch by two legs simultaneously, for what, having stepped by one leg, to pull the another to it just after the former stands on the pitch;

Drill 4 continuation

The goalkeeper catches or blocks the ball (fig. 2-4)

Fig. 2

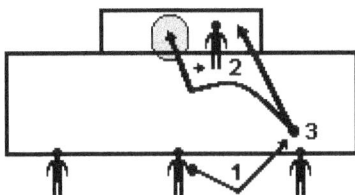

Fig. 3

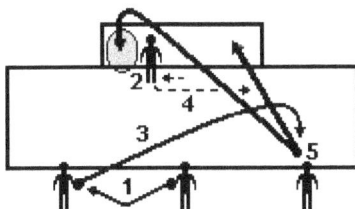

Fig. 4

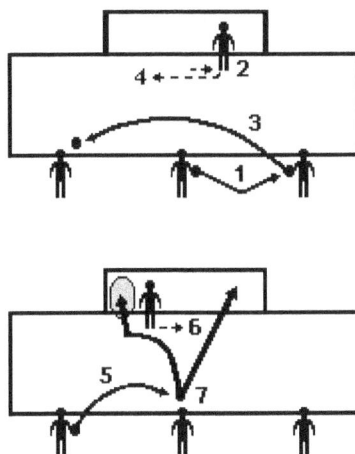

– the goalkeeper should be ready to the possible sending the ball into the net, including opposite to his movement, after every pass by his partners;

– the goalkeeper's partners should perform shots on goal from the outside of the goal area;

– the goalkeeper should switch quickly from moving to the side to catching or blocking the ball when caught wrong-footed;

– the goalkeeper may catch or block the ball when caught wrong-footed in supporting position, while diving and jumping depending in direction and speed of sending the ball by the partner

Drill 5	

Drill description	Technical tips
The coach with the ball is positioned opposite to the goal area angle 13 meters from the goal-line, one of the goalkeeper's partners – opposite to the opposite goal area angle 16 meters from the goal, while the second – opposite to the middle of the goal 16 meters from the goal-line. The goalkeeper takes position in the goal for catching and blocking the ball in case the coach shoots on goal (fig. 1). **Fig. 1** The coach send the ball with a leg across the pitch surface in parallel to the goal-line to the goalkeeper's partner positioned opposite to the middle of the goal so that he could: – perform a shot on goal with a first touch; – let the ball go through to the partner opposite to the goal area angle for performing a shot on goal with a first touch. The goalkeeper moves to the side for taking the proper position for catching or blocking the ball tacking into the account the change in its position. In different task repeats the goalkeeper's partner positioned opposite to the middle of the goal **chaotically**:	– the coach should pass the ball with such speed that it flies fast enough, though both goalkeeper's partners were comfortable to shoot on goal with a first touch; – the goalkeeper should move with sidesteps with bent legs without stepping too broadly or narrowly; – the goalkeeper should not lose contact with the pitch by two legs simultaneously, for what, having stepped by one leg, to pull the another to it just after the former stands on the pitch; – the goalkeeper has to be ready for possible sending the ball opposite to his movement to the moment when the partner shoots on goal;

Task 5 continuation

– sends the ball with a first touch in the goal area on the goalkeeper's way opposite to his movement with different trajectories; – let the ball go through to the partner, who sends it with a first touch in the goal area on the goalkeeper's way opposite to his movement with different trajectories. The goalkeeper catches or blocks the ball (fig. 2) 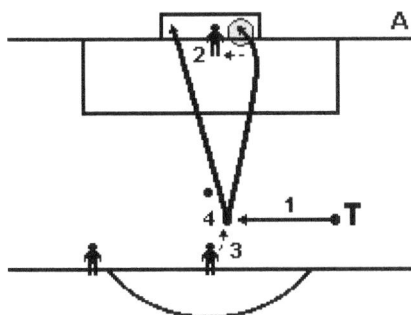 Fig. 2 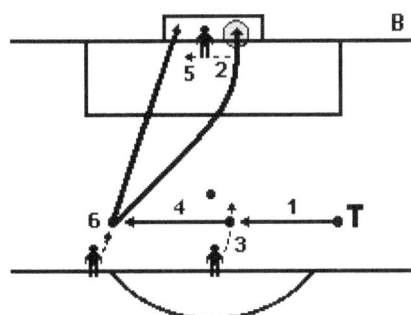	– the goalkeeper's partner who has decided to let the ball go through to the second partner instead of shooting on goal in one of task repeats should try to perform it surprisingly for the goalkeepers; – while the goalkeeper's partner lets the ball go through to the second partner instead of shooting on goal, the goalkeeper should again move to the side quickly to take the proper position for catching or blocking the ball tacking into the account the change in its position; – the goalkeeper may catch or block the ball when caught wrong-footed in supporting position, while diving and jumping depending in direction and speed of sending the ball by the partner

Drill 6	
Drill description	**Technical tips**
Two goals of standard size are mounted opposite to each other at 20 meters. Lines limiting goalkeepers' zones of actions are marked in parallel to the goal-line 4 meters from the goal. The goalkeeper is positioned at the one goal post, his partner with the ball – in the goalkeeper's zone of actions at another goal (fig. 1).	– the goalkeeper's partner may throw the ball and shoot on goal from any point of the goalkeeper's zone of actions; – the goalkeeper's partner should send the ball into the net necessarily after the goalkeeper begins to move to the side;

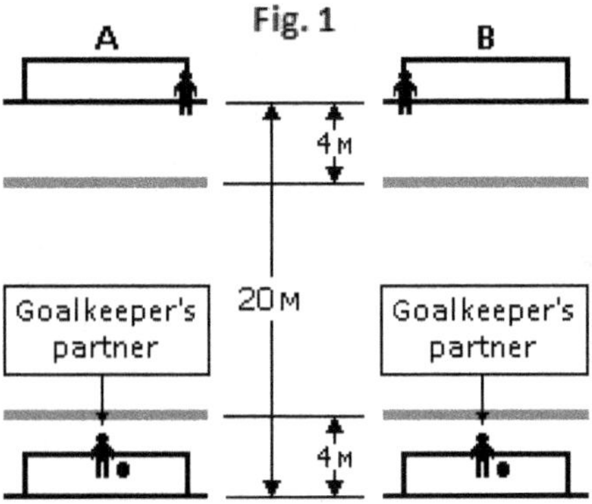

Fig. 1

The goalkeeper begins to move to the side to the middle of the goal for taking the proper position for catching or blocking the ball.

After the goalkeeper has begun move the goalkeeper's partner sends the ball **chaotically** in different repeats in the goal area on the goalkeeper's initial way of movement and opposite to his movement:

– with a throw across the pitch surface and at different heights;

– with a kick «from hands by foot» with a rebound off the pitch surface and at different heights;

– with a kick on static and moving ball («from the ground») across the pitch surface and at different heights.

– the goalkeeper should move with sidesteps with bent legs without stepping too broadly or narrowly;

– the goalkeeper should not lose contact with the pitch by two legs simultaneously, for what, having stepped by one leg, to pull the another to it just after the former stands on the pitch;

– the goalkeeper should be ready to possible sending of the ball opposite to his movement;

Drill 6 continuation

The goalkeeper catches or blocks the ball (fig. 2-4) **Fig. 2** Throwing the ball with a hand **Fig. 3** Shot from hands with a foot **Fig. 4** Shot from the ground with a foot	– the goalkeeper should switch quickly from moving to the side to catching or blocking the ball when caught wrong-footed; – the goalkeeper may catch or block the ball when caught wrong-footed in supporting position, while diving and jumping depending in direction and speed of sending the ball by the partner; – the goalkeeper and his partners may switch roles after every attempt or after series of attempts of task performance

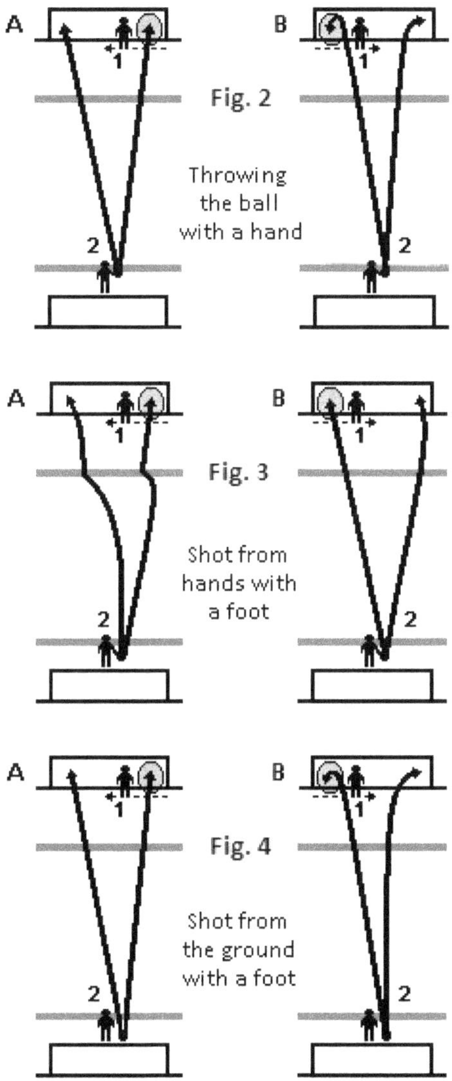

Drill 7	
Drill description	**Technical tips**
The ball is mounted in area 20 meters from the goal-line approx. opposite the goal area angle. The wall (mannequins) covering the goal area at the goal post closer relative to the ball is mounted 9 meters from the ball. The coach is positioned a few meters from the ball for shooting on goal, the goalkeeper – in the goal between the middle of the goal and the goal post distant relative to the ball for catching and blocking the ball taking into account the wall position (fig. 1). 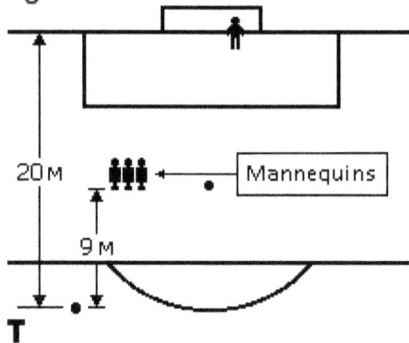 Fig. 1 20 M 9 M Mannequins T The coach begins run-up to the ball for performing a shot on goal. While the coach runs-up to the ball, the goalkeeper begins to move towards the goal post closer relative to the ball, and when the coach shoots on goal, the goalkeeper appears in position approx. in the middle of the goal while moving. The coach sends the ball **chaotically** in different task repeats in the goal area at the goalpost closer relative to the ball and opposite to the goalkeeper's movement with different trajectories.	– prior to the shooting on goal the goalkeeper should conduct the wall setup; – prior to the shooting on goal the goalkeeper should take position to see the moment of shot; – the goalkeeper should move with sidesteps with bent legs without stepping too broadly or narrowly; – the goalkeeper should not lose contact with the pitch by two legs simultaneously, for what, having stepped by one leg, to pull the another to it just after the former stands on the pitch; – the goalkeeper has to be ready for possible sending the ball opposite to his movement to the moment when the coach shoots on goal;

Task 7 continuation

The goalkeeper catches or blocks the ball (fig. 2). **Fig. 2** 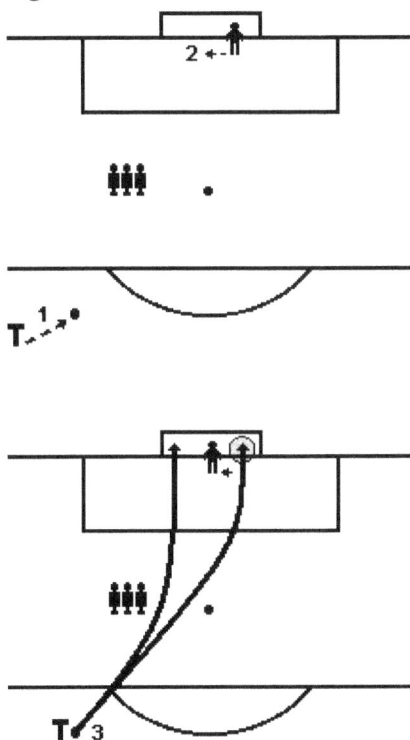 **Variant:** points of performing shots on goal by the coach are varied across the width of the pitch (at different angles to the goal)	– the goalkeeper should switch quickly from moving to the side to catching or blocking the ball when caught wrong-footed; – the goalkeeper may catch or block the ball when caught wrong-footed in supporting position, while diving and jumping depending in direction and speed of sending the ball by the coach

Drills for training catching and blocking the ball when caught wrong-footed while moving backward

Drill 1	
Drill description	**Technical tips**
Two limited spaces 10 meters long and 7 meters wide each are marked opposite to each other with short sides 8 meters from each other – the «goalkeeper's zone» and the «goalkeeper's partner zone». The goalkeeper is positioned on the line bordering the goalkeeper's zone across the width and closer to the goalkeeper's partner zone, the goalkeeper's partner with the ball – in his zone at the line closer to the goalkeeper's zone (fig. 1). Fig. 1 The goalkeeper begins to move back backwards for taking the proper position for catching or blocking the ball so that not to let it touch the pitch surface in the goalkeeper's zone in case the partner sends the ball with a mounted trajectory to this zone. After the goalkeeper begins to move **chaotically** in different task repeats his partner sends the ball with a hand into the goalkeeper's zone with a mounted trajectory so that the ball touches the pitch surface in the area behind the goalkeeper's back or in front of him.	– the goalkeeper should get in time to take such position that he could catch or reflect the ball sent both into the area behind his back and in front of him without letting the ball touch the pitch surface; – while moving back the goalkeeper may move backwards or half-sideways forward; – while moving back the goalkeeper should not step too broadly or narrowly and lose contact with the pitch by both legs simultaneously; – the goalkeeper's partner should send the ball into the goalkeeper's area timely (while the goalkeeper moving back backwards) and precisely;

Task 1 continuation

The goalkeeper catches or blocks the ball including when caught wrong-footed without letting it touch the ball in the goalkeeper's zone (fig. 2).

Fig. 2

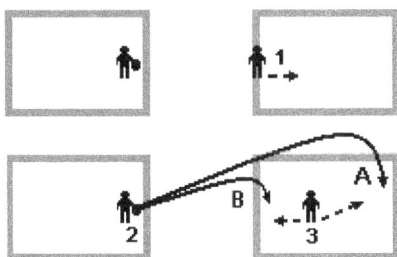

Variants:
a) points of the goalkeeper's partner position are varied across the width of goalkeeper's partner zone (fig. 3);
b) the goalkeeper's partner sends the ball into the goalkeeper's zone with a mounted trajectory with a kick «from hands by foot» (fig. 4)

Fig. 3

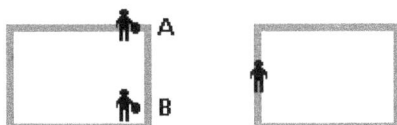

Fig. 4

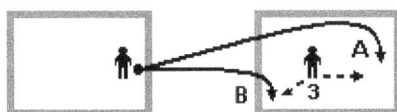

– the goalkeeper has to be ready for possible sending the ball opposite to his movement to the moment when the partner sends the ball into the goalkeeper's zone;
– the goalkeeper may catch or block the ball when caught wrong-footed in supporting position, while diving and jumping depending in direction and speed of sending the ball by the partner;
– while reflecting the ball the goalkeeper should punch it on air beyond the goalkeeper's zone;
– the goalkeeper and his partners may switch roles after every attempt or after series of attempts of task performance

Drill 2	

Drill description	Technical tips
The coach with the ball is positioned opposite to the goal 20 meters from the goal-line, the goalkeeper – on the goal area line between two mannequins mounted opposite to the goal 5 meters from each other. Bordering line 7 meters long is marked opposite to the goal in the middle of the goal are (fig. 1).	– the goalkeeper should quickly move back to the goal for taking the proper position for catching or blocking the ball in case the coach sends it into the net; – while moving back to the goal the goalkeeper may move backwards or half-sideways forward;

Fig. 1

The goalkeeper begins to move into the goal backwards to the point between the goal-line and the bordering line. After the goalkeeper reaches the bordering line the coach sends the ball with his foot into the space between mannequins with different trajectories. The goalkeepers catches or blocks the ball when caught wrong-footed without letting it get though between mannequins (fig. 2). **Variants:** a) points of the coach position are varied across the width of the pitch (fig. 3); b) points of mannequins mounting are varied across the width of the pitch within the goal area line (fig. 4)	– while moving back to the goal the goalkeeper should not step too broadly or narrowly and lose contact with the pitch by both legs simultaneously; – the goalkeeper should cross the bordering line at least with one leg; – the coach may send the ball into the space between mannequins along the pitch surface, with a rebound off the pitch surface and on air at different heights, but not higher than mannequins;

Task 2 continuation

Fig. 2

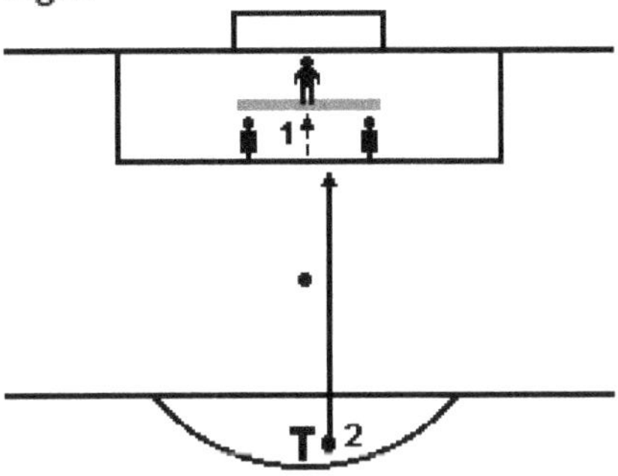

Fig. 3

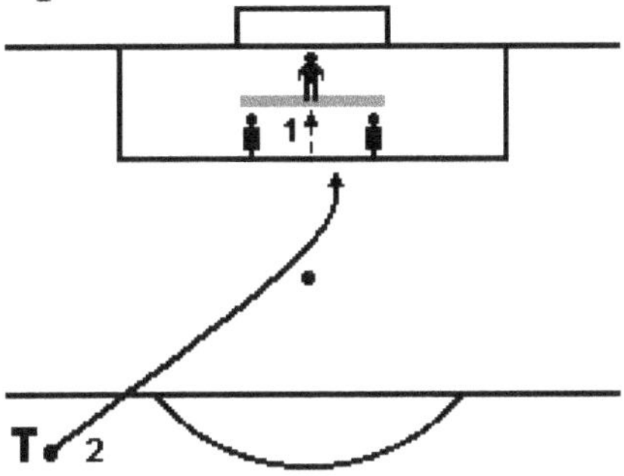

Fig. 4

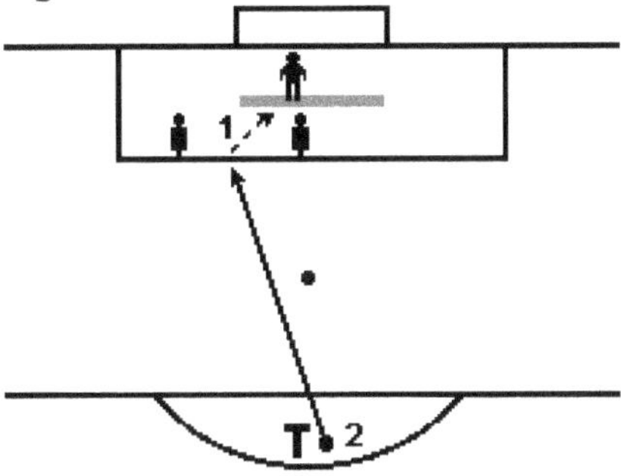

– the coach should send the ball into the space between mannequins timely;
– the coach should send the ball into the space between mannequins with such speed that catching or blocking the ball when caught wrong-footed were enforceable;
– the goalkeeper has to be ready for possible sending the ball opposite to his movement to the moment when the coach sends the ball into the space between mannequins;
– the goalkeeper may catch or block the ball when caught wrong-footed in supporting position, while diving and jumping depending in direction and speed of sending the ball by the coach

Drill 3	
Drill description	**Technical tips**
Two goalkeeper's partners are positioned on the goal area line: the one with the ball – at one angle of the goal area, the second – at the another. Bordering line 7 meters long is marked opposite to the goal in the middle of the goal area. Two mannequins are mounted on both sides of the goal area line 1 meter from it opposite to the middle of the goal. The goalkeeper takes position opposite to the middle of the goal on the goal area line (fig. 1). **Fig. 1** The goalkeeper begins to move into the goal backwards to the point between the goal-line and the bordering line. After the goalkeeper reaches the bordering line, the goalkeeper's partner with the ball sends it between mannequins to the second partner with different trajectories: – with a kick «from the ground» along the pitch surface and at different heights; – with a kick «from hands by foot» with a rebound off the pitch surface and at different heights;	– the goalkeeper should quickly move back to the goal for taking the proper position for catching or blocking the ball in case the partner sends it into the net; – while moving back to the goal the goalkeeper may move backwards or half-sideways forward; – while moving back to the goal the goalkeeper should not step too broadly or narrowly and lose contact with the pitch by both legs simultaneously; – the goalkeeper should cross the bordering line at least with one leg; – the goalkeeper's partner with the ball should send it to the second partner between mannequins timely and precisely;

Task 3 continuation

– with a throw with a rebound off the pitch surface and at different heights.

The goalkeepers catches or blocks the ball when caught wrong-footed without letting it get though between mannequins (fig. 2-4)

Fig. 2

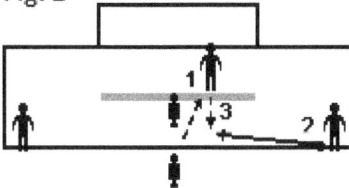

Fig. 3

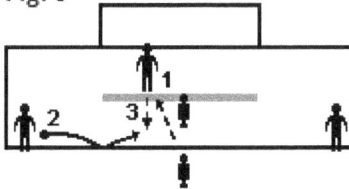

Fig. 4

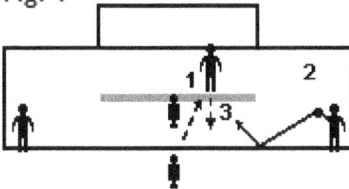

– the goalkeeper's partner with the ball should send it to the second partner with such speed that catching or blocking the ball when caught wrong-footed were enforceable;

– the goalkeeper has to be ready for possible sending the ball opposite to his movement to the moment when the partner sends the ball to the second partner;

– the goalkeeper should catch or block the ball until the moment of crossing the area between two mannequins;

– the goalkeeper may catch or block the ball when caught wrong-footed in supporting position, while diving and jumping depending in direction and speed of sending the ball by the partner

Drill 4	
Drill description	**Technical tips**
The coach with the ball is positioned between the angle of the goal area and the angle of the 18-yard box 13 meters from the goal-line, the goalkeeper's partner – opposite to the goalpost distant relative to the goalkeeper's position 6 meters from the goal-line. The goalkeeper takes position opposite to the goalpost closer to the coach's position on the goal area line (fig. 1). **Fig. 1** 13 м 6 м Goalkeeper's partner •T The goalkeeper begins to move backwards into the goal. The coach sends the ball into the net with a foot with a mounted trajectory above the goalkeeper. The goalkeeper catches or blocks the ball while moving back (fig. 2). In one of **chaotic** task repeats the coach suddenly sends the ball with a foot to the goalkeeper's partner with a mounted trajectory. The goalkeeper catches or blocks the ball when caught wrong-footed (fig. 3). **Variant:** positions of the coach, the goalkeeper and the goalkeeper's partner are varied across the width of the pitch (fig. 4)	– the goalkeeper should quickly move back to the goal for taking the proper position for catching or blocking the ball in case the coach sends it into the net; – while moving back to the goal the goalkeeper may move backwards or half-sideways forward; – while moving back to the goal the goalkeeper should not step too broadly or narrowly and lose contact with the pitch by both legs simultaneously; – the coach should send the ball into the net and to the goalkeeper's partner timely; – the coach should send the ball into the net with a mounted trajectory above the goalkeeper, while to the goalkeeper's partner with a mounted trajectory at different heights;

Task 4 continuation

Fig. 2

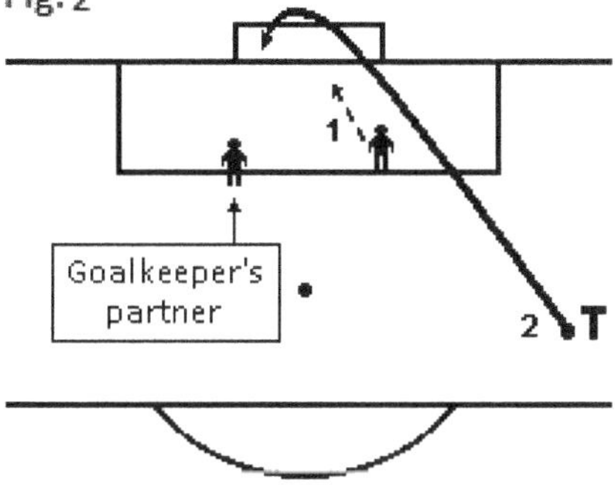

Goalkeeper's partner

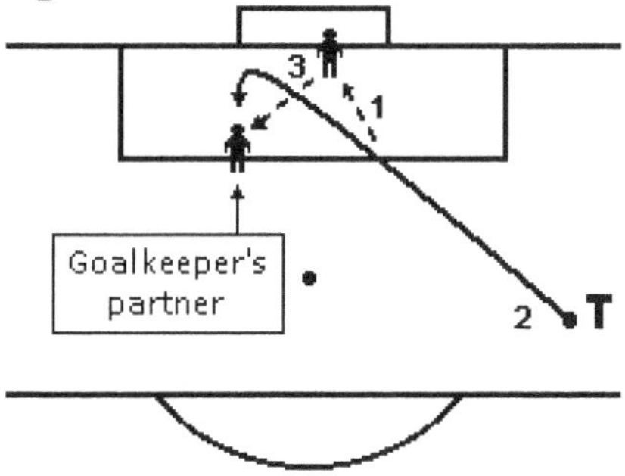

Fig. 3

Goalkeeper's partner

Fig. 4

Goalkeeper's partner

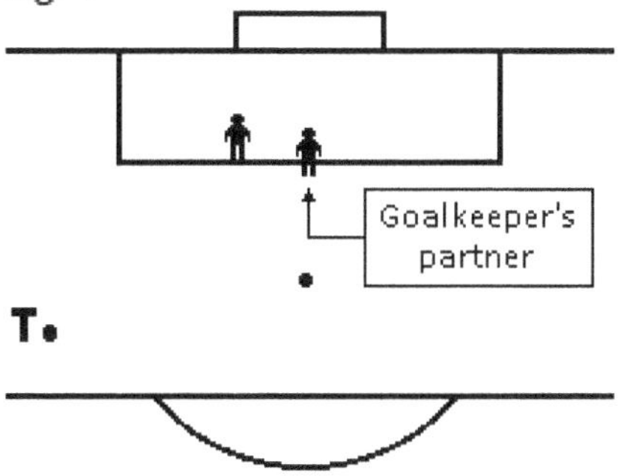

– the coach should send the ball to the goalkeeper's partner with such speed that catching or blocking the ball when caught wrong-footed were enforceable;

– the goalkeeper has to be ready for possible sending the ball opposite to his movement to the moment when the coach shoots on goal;

– the goalkeeper's partner should make a poor fight on the goalkeeper while catching or blocking the ball;

– the goalkeeper may catch or block the ball when caught wrong-footed in supporting position, while diving and jumping depending in direction and speed of sending the ball by the coach

Drill 5	
Drill description	**Technical tips**
The coach with the ball is positioned between the goal area angle and the 18-yard box angle 13 meters from the goal-line, one of the goalkeeper's partners – at the goal-line 10 meters from the goalpost closer from the coach's side, while the second – opposite to the middle of the goal 6 meters from the goal-line. The goalkeeper takes position opposite to the goalpost closer to the coach's position on the goal area line (fig. 1). 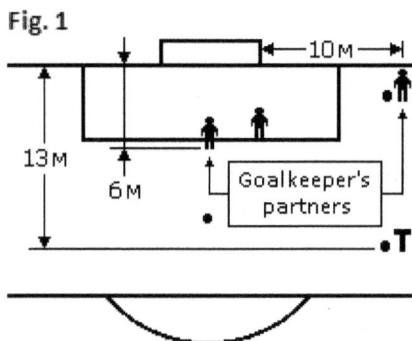 Fig. 1 The goalkeeper begins to move backwards into the goal. The coach sends the ball into the net with a foot with a mounted trajectory above the goalkeeper. The goalkeeper catches or blocks the ball while moving back (fig. 2). In one of chaotic task repeats the coach suddenly simulates a shot on goal, while the goalkeeper's partner with the ball sends it with a foot to the partner opposite to the goal. The goalkeeper catches or blocks the ball when caught wrong-footed (fig. 3).	– the goalkeeper should quickly move back to the goal for taking the proper position for catching or blocking the ball in case the coach sends it into the net; – while moving back to the goal the goalkeeper may move backwards or half-sideways forward; – while moving back to the goal the goalkeeper should not step too broadly or narrowly and lose contact with the pitch by both legs simultaneously; – the coach should send the ball into the net timely; – the coach should send the ball into the net with a mounted trajectory above the goalkeeper; – the coach should simulate shooting on goal the most authentically for the goalkeeper;

Task 5 continuation

Fig. 2

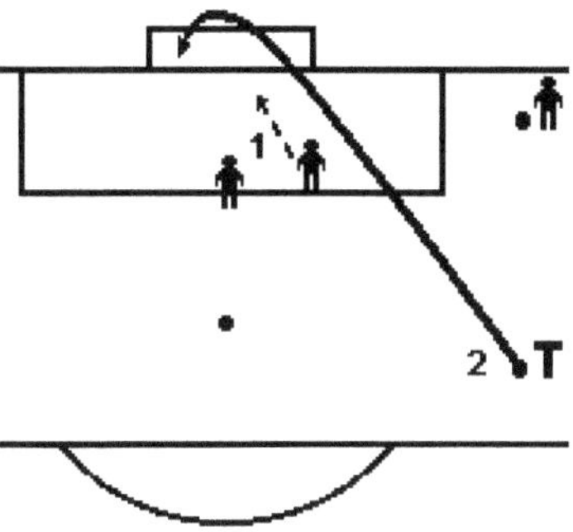

Fig. 3

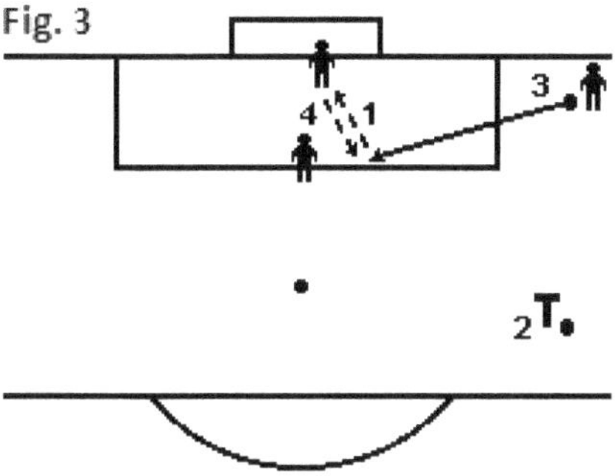

Variant: positions of the coach, the goalkeeper and the goalkeeper's partner with the ball are varied across the width of the pitch (fig. 4)

Fig. 4

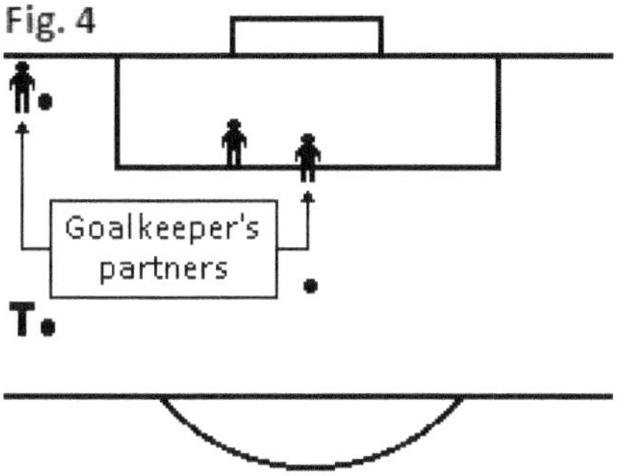

Goalkeeper's partners

– the goalkeeper's partner with the ball should send the ball to the partner timely relative to the coach's actions;

– the goalkeeper's partner with the ball may send it over the pitch surface, with a rebound off the pitch surface and on air low-level;

– on course of his movement back to the goal the goalkeeper has to be ready for possible sending the ball opposite to his movement;

– the goalkeeper should switch quickly from moving back into the goal to catching or blocking the ball when caught wrong-footed;

– the goalkeeper may catch or block the ball when caught wrong-footed in supporting position and while diving depending in direction and speed of sending the ball by the partner

Drills for training catching and blocking the ball when caught wrong-footed while moving forward

Drill 1	
Drill description	**Technical tips**
The goalkeeper is positioned in the middle of the goal, the coach with the ball in hands – opposite to the goalkeeper 20 meters from the goal-line. Bordering line 3 meters long is marked on the goal area line opposite to the middle of the goal (fig. 1).	– the goalkeeper should cross the bordering line at least with one leg; – the goalkeeper should move forward with a normal run at first, and with sidesteps near the bordering line;
Fig. 1 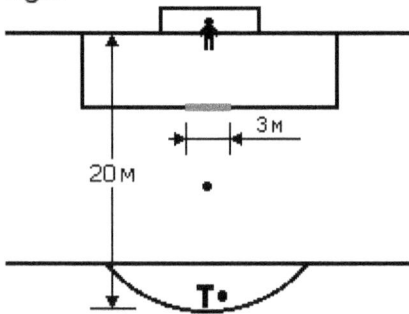	– while moving with sidesteps the goalkeeper should not step too broadly or narrowly and lose contact with the pitch by both legs simultaneously;
The goalkeeper begins to move quickly to the point right beyond the bordering line. After the goalkeeper reaches the bordering line the coach sends the ball with a kick «from hands by foot» into the net with a mounted trajectory. The goalkeeper catches or blocks the ball when caught wrong-footed (fig. 2). **Variants:** a) points of performing shots on goal by the coach are varied across the width of the pitch (fig. 3); b) points of marking of the bordering line on the goal area line are varied across the width of the pitch (fig. 4)	– the goalkeeper has to be ready for possible sending the ball opposite to his movement to the moment when the coach shoots on goal; – the coach should send the ball opposite to the goalkeeper's movement with a mounted trajectory timely and precisely;

Task 1 continuation

Fig. 2 **Fig. 3** **Fig. 4** 	– the goalkeeper should quickly change the direction of movement to the opposite and quickly move back to the goal; – while moving back to the goal the goalkeeper may move backwards or half-sideways forward; – the goalkeeper may catch or block the ball when caught wrong-footed in supporting position, while diving and jumping depending in direction and speed of sending the ball by the coach

Drill 2	
Drill description	**Technical tips**
The coach with the ball is positioned opposite to the goal 16 meters from the goal-line, two goalkeeper's partners with the ball – opposite to the goal on the goal area line 5 meters from each other. The goalkeeper takes position in the goal for catching or blocking the ball in case the coach shoots on goal (fig. 1). **Fig. 1** The coach sends the ball with a foot to one of the goalkeeper's partners with different trajectories and medium speed. The goalkeeper tries to knock out the ball as far as possible in the area in front of the partner. As soon as the goalkeeper or his partner to whom the ball has been sent touches the ball, the another goalkeeper's partner sends his ball with a foot to the coach over the pitch surface. The goalkeeper immediately begins to move back to the goal, while the coach sends the ball with his foot into the net with a mounted trajectory. The goalkeeper catches or blocks the ball when caught wrong-footed (fig. 2). **Variant:** points of performance passes and shots on goal by the coach are varied across the width and along the length of the pitch (fig. 3)	– the coach should send the ball to one of the goalkeeper's partners within such range of speed that blocking the ball by the goalkeeper was enforceable; – the coach should vary trajectories of sending the ball to one of the goalkeeper's partners in different task repeats; – the goalkeeper should be ready for sending the ball by the coach to one of partners with different trajectories; – the goalkeeper should try to knock out the ball sent by the coach to one of partners beyond the 18-yard box; – the goalkeeper may block the ball sent by the coach to one of partners in supporting position, while diving and jumping;

Task 2 continuation

Fig. 2

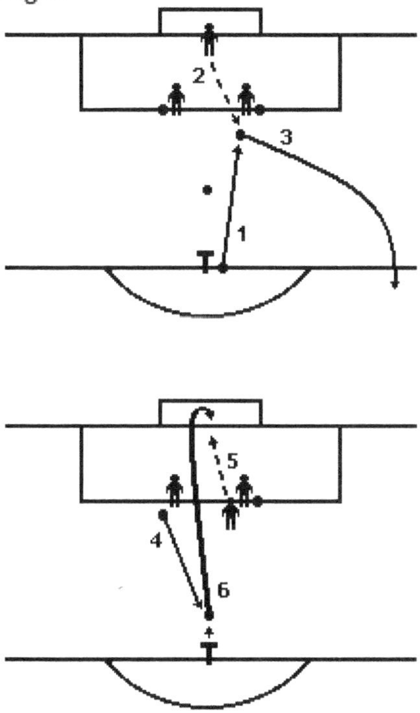

Fig. 3

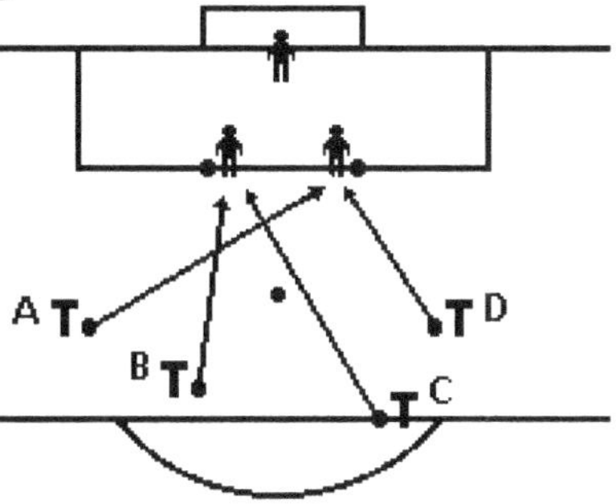

– the goalkeeper's partner to whom the coach has sent the ball should catch it in case the goalkeeper is unable to block it;
– the goalkeeper's partner to whom the coach hasn't pass the ball should send his ball to the coach timely and precisely for him to shoot on goal;
– the coach should send the ball into the net precisely with a mounted trajectory above the goalkeeper;
– while moving back to the goal the goalkeeper may move backwards or half-sideways forward;
– the goalkeeper may catch or block the ball when caught wrong-footed in supporting position, while diving and jumping depending in direction and speed of sending the ball by the coach

Drill 3	
Drill description	**Technical tips**
The coach with the ball is situated between the 18-yard box corner and the sideline 20 meters from the goal-line, one goalkeeper's partner – opposite to the middle of the goal 8 meters from the goal-line, second and third partners – opposite to the middle of the goal 6 meters from the goal-line and 2 meters from each other. The goalkeeper takes position 2-3 meters from the goal-line approx. opposite to the middle of the goal (fig. 1). **Fig.1** 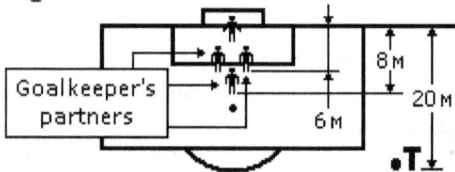 The coach sends the ball with a foot to the goalkeeper's partner positioned 8 meters from the goal-line with a mounted trajectory. The goalkeeper moves towards the partner positioned 8 meters from the goal-line and catches or blocks the ball. In one of chaotic task repeats the goalkeeper's partners positioned 6 meters from the goal-line suddenly join hands with one hand after he begins to move for catching or blocking the ball, blocking his way to the ball. In this case the goalkeeper begins to move back to the goal immediately, while his partner positioned 8 meters from the goal-line catches the ball and throws it to the goal with a mounted trajectory. The goalkeeper catches or blocks the ball when caught wrong-footed (fig. 2).	– in case the goalkeeper's partners positioned 6 meters from the goal-line decided no to block his way to the ball, they should act passive towards the goalkeeper; – in case the goalkeeper's partners positioned 6 meters from the goal-line didn't block his way to the ball, the goalkeeper should try to catch or block the ball; – in case the goalkeeper's partners positioned 6 meters from the goal-line didn't block his way to the ball, the goalkeeper's partner positioned 8 meters from the goal-line should make a poor fight on him while catching or blocking the ball;

Task 3 continuation

Fig. 2

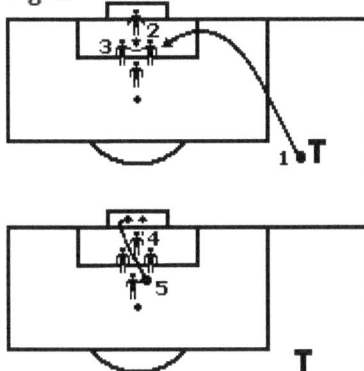

Variants:
a) points of performance passes by the coach are varied across the width and along the length of the pitch (fig. 3);

Fig. 3

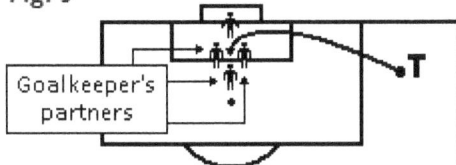

b) the goalkeeper's partners are positioned at the goal area corners closer and distant relative to the point of the pass (fig. 4)

Fig. 4

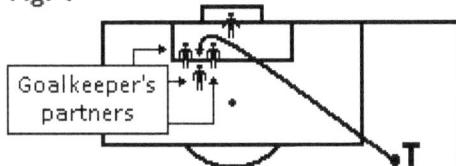

– in case the goalkeeper's partners positioned 6 meters from the goal-line decided to block his way to the ball, they should try to do it suddenly after the goalkeeper makes several steps to the ball;

– in case if the goalkeeper's partners positioned 6 meters from the goal-line have blocked his way to the ball, the goalkeeper should change the direction of movement to the opposite and move back to the goal quickly;

– in case the goalkeeper's partners positioned 6 meters from the goal-line have blocked his way to the ball, the goalkeeper's partner positioned 8 meters from the goal-line should obligingly catch the ball and send it to the goal with hand with a mounted trajectory above the goalkeeper quickly and precisely

Drill 4	
Drill description	**Technical tips**
The coach with the ball is positioned between the corner of the 18-yard box and the sideline 25 meters from the goal-line, one goalkeeper's partner – opposite to the goalpost distant relative to the goalkeeper's position 6 meters from the goal-line, and another – at the penalty spot. The goalkeeper takes position 2-3 meters from the goal-line approx. opposite to the middle of the goal (fig. 1). **Fig. 1** The coach sends the ball with his foot to the goalkeeper's partner positioned at the goalpost distant relative to the coach's position with a high mounted trajectory. The goalkeeper moves forward and catches or blocks the ball (fig. 2). In one of chaotic task repeats the goalkeeper's partner positioned at the penalty spot suddenly catches the ball and throws it to the goal with a mounted trajectory after the coach performs a pass. Having begun to move towards the partner positioned at the goalpost distant relative to the coach's position, the goalkeeper catches or blocks the ball when caught wrong-footed (fig. 3).	– the coach should send the ball to the goalkeeper's partner positioned opposite to the goalpost distant relative to the coach's position so that the goalkeeper's partner positioned at the penalty spot can catch the ball; – the goalkeeper's partner positioned at the goalpost distant relative to the coach's position should make a poor fight on the goalkeeper while catching or blocking the ball; – in case the goalkeeper's partner positioned at the penalty spot decided to catch the ball, he should to do it surprisingly for the goalkeeper;

Task 4 continuation

Fig. 2

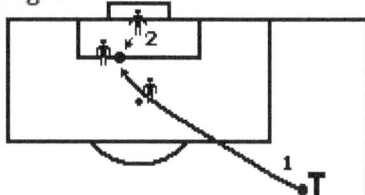

Fig. 3

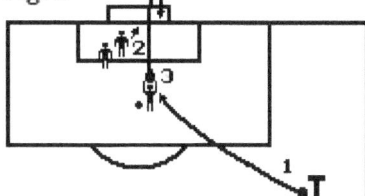

Variant: points of position of the coach and the goalkeeper's partner on the same line are varied relative to the goal (fig. 4 and 5)

Fig. 4

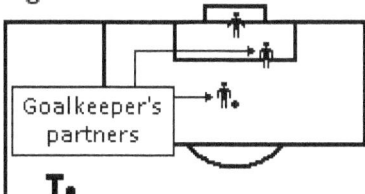

Fig. 5

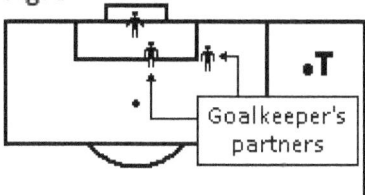

– in case the goalkeeper's partner positioned at the penalty spot has caught the ball, the goalkeeper should quickly change the direction of movement to the opposite and quickly move back to the goal;

– while moving back to the goal the goalkeeper may move backwards or half-sideways forward;

– in case the goalkeeper's partner positioned at the penalty spot has caught the ball, he should throw it to the goal with a mounted trajectory above the goalkeeper quickly and precisely;

– the goalkeeper may catch or block the ball when caught wrong-footed in supporting position, while diving and jumping depending in direction and speed of sending the ball by the partner

Drill 5	
Drill description	**Technical tips**
The coach with the ball is positioned 1 meter from the goalpost beyond the goal-line, the goalkeeper's partner – at the penalty spot. Two mannequins are mounted opposite to the middle of the goal on the goal area line 3 meters from each other. The goalkeeper takes position 2 meters from the goal-line approx. opposite to the middle of the goal (fig. 1). Fig. 1 The coach sends the ball to the goalkeeper's partner with a rebound off the pitch surface so that he could send with his head into the net or into the space between mannequins. The goalkeeper moves forward for taking the proper position for catching or blocking the ball in case it is sent into the net or into the space between mannequins. The goalkeeper's partner sends the ball with his head into the goal with a mounted trajectory and into the space between mannequins with different trajectories in different task repeats **chaotically.** The goalkeepers catches or blocks the ball without letting it get though between mannequins and into the net (fig. 2).	– the coach should send the ball to the goalkeeper's partner so that he could send the ball with his head into the goal or into the space between mannequins from the distance no closer than 9 meters from the goal-line; – after a pass from the coach to the goalkeeper's partner the goalkeeper should get in time to take position to be able to catch or block the ball sent both into the net and into the space between mannequins; – the goalkeeper's partner should send the ball into the space between mannequins not higher than them, while into the net – with a mounted trajectory above the goalkeeper;

Task 5 continuation

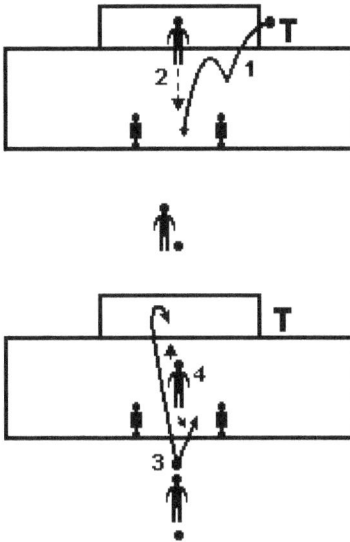

Fig. 2

— the goalkeeper may catch or block the ball when caught wrong-footed in supporting position, while diving and jumping depending in direction and speed of sending the ball into the net by the partner

Variant: points of mannequins mounting are varied across the width of the pitch within the goal area line, while points of the goalkeeper's partner position is varied across the width of the pitch up to 5 meters to the left and to the right relative to the penalty spot (fig. 3)

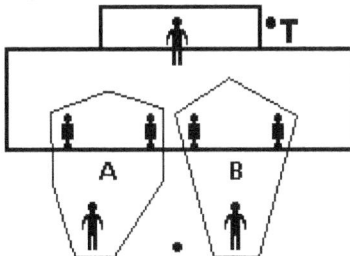

Fig. 3

71

5. 3. A set of special exercises for training catching and blocking the ball when caught wrong-footed by goalkeepers in case of change of the ball trajectory on course of flight towards the goal

Drills for training catching and blocking the ball when caught wrong-footed during its motion in new direction over the pitch surface

Drill 1	
Drill description	**Technical tips**
The coach with the ball is positioned opposite to the middle of the goal 16 meters from the goal-line, the goalkeeper's partner with the ball – 10 meters from the goal-line at the nominal line between the coach's position and the goalpost. The goalkeeper takes position in the goal for catching or blocking the ball in case the coach shoots on goal (fig. 1). Fig. 1 10 M Goalkeeper's partner T. The coach sends the ball with a foot into the goal corner covered by the goalkeeper's partner over the pitch surface, while the goalkeeper's partner doesn't prevent the ball from moving into the net.	– the coach should precisely send the ball over the pitch surface into the goal corner, covered by the goalkeeper's partner; – on course of actions on catching or blocking the ball sent by the coach the goalkeeper should be ready for possible ball ricochet; – if the goalkeeper's partner decided not to stop or block the ball sent by the coach, he should reduce the visibility for the goalkeeper to the greatest extent;

Task 1 continuation

The goalkeeper catches or blocks the ball (fig. 2).

Fig. 2

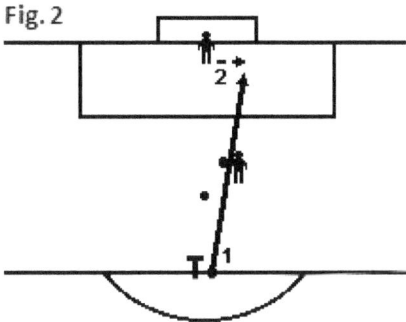

In one of chaotic task repeats the goalkeeper's partner suddenly stops or reflects with a foot the ball sent by the coach into the corner of the goal, and immediately sends his ball into the opposite corner over the pitch surface.

Having started actions for catching or blocking the ball sent by the coach, the goalkeeper catches or blocks the ball, sent by the partner, when caught wrong-footed (fig. 3).

Fig. 3

Variant: positions of the coach and the goalkeeper's partner covering the corner of the goal are varied across the width of the pitch

– in case the goalkeeper's partner decided to catch or block the ball sent by the coach, he should do it surprisingly for the goalkeeper;

– after stopping or reflecting the ball sent by the coach the goalkeeper's partner has to send his ball into the net without a delay;

– the goalkeeper's partner should precisely send the ball opposite to the goalkeeper's actions on catching or blocking the ball sent by the coach so that catching or blocking the ball when caught wrong-footed were enforceable;

– the goalkeeper should switch quickly from performing actions on catching or blocking the ball sent by the coach to catching or blocking the ball, sent by the partner, when caught wrong-footed

Drill 2	

Drill description	Technical tips
The coach with the ball is positioned opposite to the goalpost 16 meters from the goal-line. The reflecting panel 0,5 meters high and 2 meters long is mounted opposite to the goal perpendicularly to the goal-line so that its edge closer to the goal was on the nominal line between the ball and the goalpost distant relative to the coach 8 meters from the goal-line. The goalkeeper takes position in the goal for catching or blocking the ball in case the coach shoots on goal (fig. 1).	– in case the coach has decided to send the ball into the net without a ricochet, he should send the ball over the pitch surface into the distant corner of the goal; – on course of actions on catching or blocking the ball sent by the coach in the distant relative to him corner of the goal the goalkeeper should be ready for possible change of direction of the ball as a result of touching the reflecting panel;

Fig. 1

The coach sends the ball into the distant corner of the goal over the pitch surface so that the was flying near the edge of the reflecting panel. The goalkeeper catches or blocks the ball (fig. 2). In one of **chaotic** task repeats the coach suddenly sends the ball over the pitch surface towards the distant goalpost so that it touched the edge of the reflecting panel and bounced into the corner of the goal closer relative to the coach.	– in case the coach has decided to send the ball into the net with a ricochet, he should try to send the ball over the pitch surface as close to the closer relative to the goal edge of the reflecting panel as possible;

Task 2 continuation

Having begun actions on catching or blocking the ball flying initially towards the corner of the goal distant relative to the coach, the goalkeeper catches or blocks the ball, that has changed the direction of movement as a result of touching the reflecting panel, when caught wrong-footed (fig. 3).

Fig. 2

Fig. 3

Variant: points of the coach's position and the reflecting panel mounting are varied so that its edge closer to the goal was at the line of the ball movement when it's sent to the distant corner of the goal by the coach

– the coach should send the ball to the reflecting panel with such speed that catching or blocking the ball when caught wrong-footed were enforceable;

– the goalkeeper should switch quickly from performing actions on catching or blocking the ball before it touches the reflecting panel to catching or blocking the ball, bounced off the reflecting panel, when caught wrong-footed;

– the goalkeeper may catch or block the ball when caught wrong-footed in supporting position and while diving depending on stage of actions on catching and blocking the ball before it touches the reflecting panel, direction and speed of sending the ball after its bounce off the reflecting panel

Drills for training catching and blocking the ball when caught wrong-footed during its motion in new direction with a bounce off the pitch surface

Drill 1	
Drill description	**Technical tips**
The coach with the ball is positioned opposite to the goal 20 meters from the goal-line, two goalkeeper's partners (one with the ball) – at the penalty spot on the nominal line between the coach's position and the goalpost. The goalkeeper takes position in the goal for catching or blocking the ball in case the coach shoots on goal (fig. 1). **Fig. 1** The coach sends the ball with a foot into the goal corner, covered by the goalkeeper's partners, with a high speed, while the goalkeeper's partners don't prevent the ball from moving into the net. The goalkeeper catches or blocks the ball (fig. 2). In one of chaotic task repeats the goalkeeper's partner without the ball suddenly catches or reflects the ball sent by the coach into the corner of the goal, while the second partner immediately sends his ball into the opposite corner of the goal with a rebound off the pitch surface.	– the coach should precisely send the ball with different trajectories into the goal corner, covered by the goalkeeper's partners; – on course of actions on catching or blocking the ball sent by the coach the goalkeeper should be ready for possible ball ricochet; – if the goalkeeper's partner without the ball decided not to catch or block the ball sent by the coach, he should reduce the visibility for the goalkeeper to the greatest extent; – in case the goalkeeper's partner without the ball decided to catch or block the ball sent by the coach, he should do it surprisingly for the goalkeeper;

Task 1 continuation

Having started actions for catching or blocking the ball sent by the coach, the goalkeeper catches or blocks the ball, sent by the partner, when caught wrong-footed (fig. 3).

Fig. 2

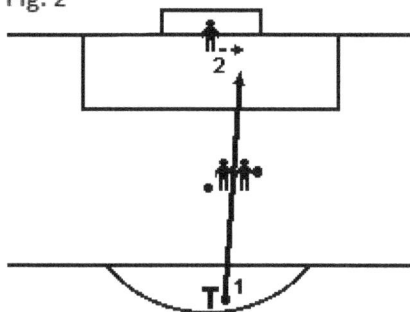

Fig. 3

Variants:

a) points of position of the coach and the goalkeeper's partners are varied across the width of the pitch so that they cover the direction of the ball sent into the net by the coach;

b) points of position of the coach and the goalkeeper's partners are varied along the length of the pitch so that they both can and cannot prevent the ball from moving into the net

– the goalkeeper's partner with the ball should reduce the visibility for the goalkeeper to the greatest extent and be ready to send his ball into the net;

– after the goalkeeper's partner caught or reflected the ball sent by the coach the second partner has to send his ball into the net without a delay;

– the goalkeeper's partner should precisely send the ball opposite to the goalkeeper's actions on catching or blocking the ball sent by the coach so that catching or blocking the ball when caught wrong-footed were enforceable;

– the goalkeeper should switch quickly from performing actions on catching or blocking the ball sent by the coach to catching or blocking the ball, sent by the partner, when caught wrong-footed

Drill 2	
Drill description	**Technical tips**
The coach with the ball is positioned opposite to the middle of the goal 13 meters from the goal-line, two goalkeeper's partners – 7 meters from the goal-line: one on the nominal line between the coach's position and the right goalpost, the another – on the nominal line between the coach's position and the left goalpost. The goalkeeper takes position in the goal for catching or blocking the ball in case the coach shoots on goal (fig. 1). **Fig. 1** The coach sends the ball with a foot into the left and the right goal corners on air at medium height and speed, while the goalkeeper's partners don't prevent the ball from moving into the net. The goalkeeper catches or blocks the ball (fig. 2). In one of chaotic task repeats the goalkeeper's partner suddenly reflects the ball, sent by the coach into the corner of the goal, with a hand or hands so that it ricocheted to the opposite corner of the goal with a rebound off the pitch surface.	– the coach should send the ball on air to the goal corners precisely; – on course of actions on catching or blocking the ball sent by the coach the goalkeeper should be ready for possible ball ricochet; – if the goalkeeper's partner decided not to change the direction of the ball sent by the coach, he should reduce the visibility for the goalkeeper to the greatest extent; – in case the goalkeeper's partner decided to change the direction the ball sent by the coach, he should do it surprisingly for the goalkeeper;

78

Task 2 continuation

Having started actions for catching or blocking the ball sent by the coach, the goalkeeper catches or blocks the ball, reflected by the partner, when caught wrong-footed (fig. 3). **Fig. 2** 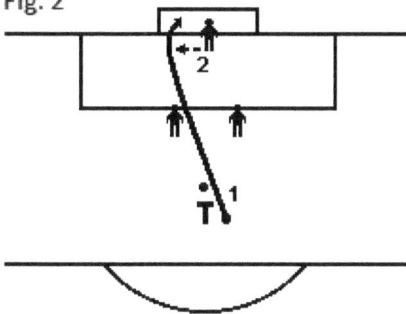 **Fig. 3** 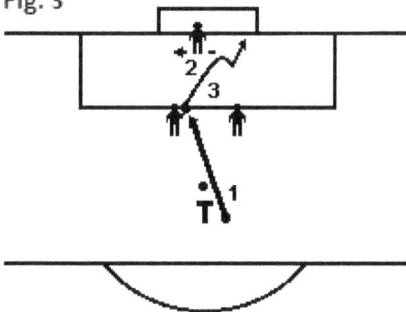 **Variants:** a) points of position of the coach and the goalkeeper's partners are varied across the width of the pitch so that they cover the direction of the ball sent into the goal corners by the coach; b) points of position of the goalkeeper's partners are varied along the length of the pitch so that they could send the ball into the net with a rebound off the pitch surface	– in case the goalkeeper's partner decided to change the direction of the ball flying into the net, he should precisely send it opposite to the goalkeeper's actions on catching or blocking the ball sent by the coach so that catching or blocking the ball when caught wrong-footed were enforceable; – the goalkeeper may catch or block the ball when caught wrong-footed in supporting position and while diving depending on stage of actions on catching and blocking the ball sent by the coach, direction and speed of the ball after reflecting by the partner

Drills for training catching and blocking the ball when caught wrong-footed during its motion in new direction on air at different heights

Drill 1	
Drill description	**Technical tips**
The coach with the ball is positioned opposite to the goal 20 meters from the goal-line, two goalkeeper's partners (one with the ball) – at the penalty spot on the nominal line between the coach's position and the goalpost. The goalkeeper takes position in the goal for catching or blocking the ball in case the coach shoots on goal (fig. 1). **Fig. 1** The coach sends the ball with a foot into the goal corner, covered by the goalkeeper's partners, with a high speed on air, while the goalkeeper's partners don't prevent the ball from moving into the net. The goalkeeper catches or blocks the ball (fig. 2). In one of chaotic task repeats the goalkeeper's partner without the ball suddenly catches or reflects the ball sent by the coach into the corner of the goal, while the second partner immediately sends his ball into the opposite corner of the goal on air.	– the coach should precisely send the ball on air into the goal corner, covered by the goalkeeper's partners; – on course of actions on catching or blocking the ball sent by the coach the goalkeeper should be ready for possible ball ricochet; – if the goalkeeper's partner without the ball decided not to catch or block the ball sent by the coach, he should reduce the visibility for the goalkeeper to the greatest extent; – in case the goalkeeper's partner without the ball decided to catch or block the ball sent by the coach, he should do it surprisingly for the goalkeeper;

Task 1 continuation

Having started actions for catching or blocking the ball sent by the coach, the goalkeeper catches or blocks the ball, sent by the partner, when caught wrong-footed (fig. 3).

Fig. 2

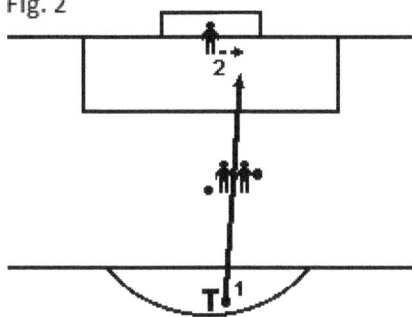

Fig. 3

Variants:

a) points of position of the coach and the goalkeeper's partners are varied across the width of the pitch so that they cover the direction of the ball sent into the net by the coach;

b) points of position of the coach and the goalkeeper's partners are varied along the length of the pitch so that they both can and cannot prevent the ball from moving into the net

– the goalkeeper's partner with the ball should reduce the visibility for the goalkeeper to the greatest extent and be ready to send his ball into the net;

– after the goalkeeper's partner caught or reflected the ball sent by the coach the second partner has to send his ball into the net without a delay;

– the goalkeeper's partner should precisely send the ball opposite to the goalkeeper's actions on catching or blocking the ball sent by the coach so that catching or blocking the ball when caught wrong-footed were enforceable;

– the goalkeeper should switch quickly from performing actions on catching or blocking the ball sent by the coach to catching or blocking the ball, sent by the partner, when caught wrong-footed

Drill 2	

Drill description	Technical tips
The coach with the ball is positioned opposite to the middle of the goal 16 meters from the goal-line.	– if the coach decided to send the ball into the net without ricochet, he should try to send it lowly above the pitch surface;
Four tubes of a light metal 2 meters long each and with diameter equal to goalposts diameter (12 cm) are laid zigzag back to back opposite to the goal across its width 6-7 meters from the goal-line on the pitch surface.	
The goalkeeper takes position in the goal for catching or blocking the ball in case the coach shoots on goal (fig. 1).	– on course of actions on catching or blocking the ball sent by the coach lowly above the pitch surface the goalkeeper should be ready for possible change of direction of the ball as a result of touching one of tubes;

Fig. 1

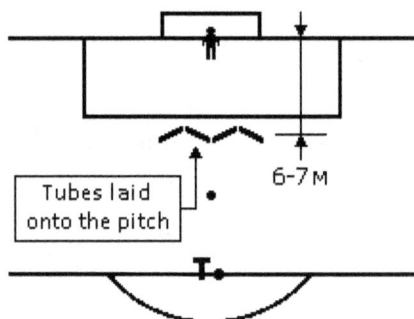

Tubes laid onto the pitch

6-7 M

The coach sends the ball into the net with a foot with a high speed on air low-level and with a rebound off the pitch surface so that the ball doesn't touch tubes, performing shots: – «from the ground»; – «from hands». The goalkeeper catches or blocks the ball (fig. 2). In one of chaotic task repeats the coach suddenly sends the ball into the net over the pitch surface with a high speed so that it touches one of tubes.	– in case the coach has decided to send the ball into the net with a ricochet, he should send the ball over the pitch surface with a high speed so that it doesn't overleap tubes;

Task 2 continuation

After touching the tube the ball changes the initial direction of movement and bounces into the net on air with unpredictable trajectory.

Having begun actions on catching or blocking the ball sent by the coach in definite direction, the goalkeeper catches or blocks the ball, that has changed the direction of movement as a result of touching the tube, when caught wrong-footed (fig. 3).

Fig. 2

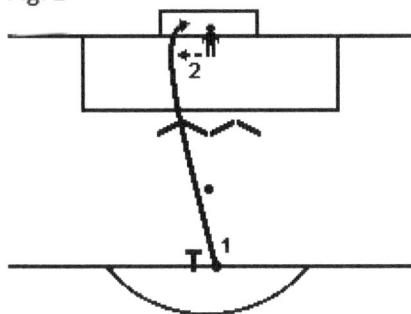

Fig. 3

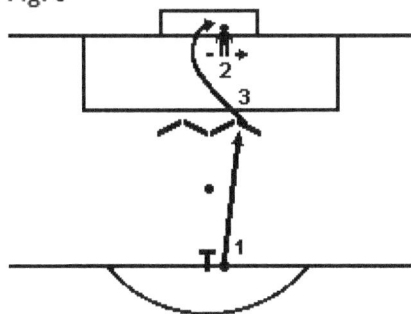

Variant: points of the coach's position and lying of tubes are varied across the width and along the length of the pitch relative to the goal

– the goalkeeper should switch quickly from performing actions on catching or blocking the ball before it touches one of tubes to catching or blocking the ball, changed the direction of movement as a result of touching one of tubes, when caught wrong-footed;

– the goalkeeper may catch or block the ball when caught wrong-footed in supporting position and while diving depending on stage of actions on catching and blocking the ball before it touches one of panels, direction and speed of sending the ball after its bounce off one of panels

CHAPTER 6.
DRILLS FOR IN-FIELD PLAYERS SUGGESTING THE POSSIBILITY TO TRAIN CATCHING AND BLOCKING THE BALL WHEN CAUGHT WRONG-FOOTED BY GOALKEEPERS

6. 1. Kinds of exercises for training of scoring goals by players

Participation in drills designed for in-field players, mainly in drills for perfection of technique and tactics of scoring goals, takes considerable time of goalkeepers' training time.

Possibilities of training catching and blocking the ball when caught wrong-footed by goalkeepers in these drills are due firstly to how the attack finishing is going on.

All drills in which in-field players perform shots on goal may be divided into two types, differ in the degree of premeditation and improvisation of players' actions in conclusion of scoring episodes, exactly finishing normally or variativelly.

In normally finishing drills the point and manner of shooting on goal and actions on delivering the ball to the shooting positions are specified in advance.

Variativelly finishing exercises are defined by the ability of in-field players to act with a greater or lesser variability both technically and tactically.

Amongst these drills there are such, in which players should choose the most rational decision on how to act from two or three possible during the conclusion of attacking actions, though they must begin each attack beginning in the same standard conditions.

The other part of variativelly finishing drills presents various variants of football game (gaming drills), in which episodes of scoring begin and finish by players fully depending on situation.

From the point of view of perfection of catching and blocking the ball when caught wrong-footed by goalkeepers more efficient are those drill for training in-field players, which conditions suggest the uncertainty of time and place of shooting on goal and who would perform it, i.e. variativelly finishing drills.

6. 2. Methods of increasing the number of goalkeepers' actions on catching and blocking the ball when caught wrong-footed in exercises for training of scoring goals by players

In normally beginning drills for training scoring goals by players the increasing of number of goalkeepers' actions on catching and blocking the ball when caught wrong-footed is possible on the following conditions of these drills organization.

First. If a player moving with the ball may shoot on goal randomly at time and place on the pitch.

Second. If the ball can be sent in different areas of the pitch during a pass leading to the finishing shot.

Third. If a shot on goal may be performed by one of two or three players participating in certain episode of goalscoring.

While performing gaming drills goalkeepers are in specialized conditions, and so these drills may be considered the most effective training resources for perfection of various actions on catching and blocking the ball, including when caught wrong-footed, by goalkeepers, if they could perform a large amount of such actions in these drills.

Number of cases of catching and blocking the ball by goalkeepers when caught wrong-footed on course of gaming drills may be increased using special organization of these drills, exactly providing football games in the small area of the pitch with contiguous goals of standard size, protected by goalkeepers, and little number of in-field players in teams.

In this case specialized conditions from the point of view of specificity of performing actions with the ball by players within the 18-yard box and nearby in competitive games are provided. This allows goalkeepers to train catching and blocking the ball when caught wrong-footed in the context of perfection of the main specific goalkeeper anticipation reactions:

– anticipation of development of play situations;

– anticipation of moment, speed and direction of sending the ball on the player's movements;

– anticipation of point and moment of coming into contact with the ball along its trajectory.

It has to be noted that while organization of drill «game with the contiguous goals» using certain methodological technique there can be provided conditions for training not only attacking and defending actions technique, but also a wide range of individual and group tactical actions, and also the working load coming to players may be regulated.

With that the spontaneous increasing of number of one or another goalkeepers' actions on catching and blocking the ball when caught wrong-footed in different situations: when goalkeepers move before the moment of sending the ball into the net and when the trajectory of the ball flying into the net is suddenly changed as a result of a touch by the player.

Next consider how some methodological techniques of organization of gaming drills with the contiguous goals, applied for increasing number and expanding range of actions with the ball performed by players, may certainly affect goalkeepers' actions on catching and blocking the ball when caught wrong-footed (table 1).

Following are sets of gaming drills with the contiguous goals for training catching and blocking the ball when caught wrong-footed by goalkeepers in different situations.

Table 1. The impact of methodological techniques of organization of gaming drills with the contiguous goals, applied for increasing of number and variety of players' actions with the ball, one the structure of the game and goalkeeper's actions on catching and blocking the ball when caught wrong-footed

Methodological techniques	How impact on the structure of the game and goalkeepers' actions
Change of the playing ground size	It is possible to provide the congestion of players in certain areas – the probability of goalkeepers playing when caught wrong-footed in case of ricochets of the ball is higher
Change of the playing ground shape	On the short and wide pitch there are more passes and movements with the ball across the width of the pitch – goalkeepers play when caught wrong-footed while moving to the side more often
Change of position of goal mounting	Diagonal mounting of the goal suggests passes at sufficiently long distance – the possibility of goalkeepers playing when caught wrong-footed is higher while moving forward and backward
Varying the number of players in drill	If number of players in teams is too large, the number of goalscoring episodes decreases, so lower the possibility of goalkeepers playing when caught wrong-footed
Stimulating players to perform some actions with the ball	Encouraging players for shooting on goal with a first touch results in increasing of number of such actions – goalkeepers play when caught wrong-footed while moving to the side more often
Introduction of restrictions on performing some actions with the ball by players	Restricting the number of passes by players from the one team to each other and time of possession by the team in specific attack results in increasing of number of goalscoring episodes – possibility of goalkeepers playing when caught wrong-footed is higher

6. 3. Set of gaming drills with the contiguous goals for training of goalscoring by players with increased number of goalkeepers' actions on catching and blocking the ball when caught wrong-footed

Drills for training catching and blocking the ball when caught wrong-footed by goalkeepers in case of movement before the moment of sending the ball towards the goal

Drill 1	
Drill description	**Technical tips**
One on one play. Pitch size: 10 meters long, 12 meters wide. Goalkeepers put the ball into play after catching it or when it crosses the goal-line and sidelines. Players are permitted to pass the ball to goalkeepers only when putting it into play after fouls. Corners are not awarded. Offsides are not given. Goal scored at the rebound counts as two. Play time in one repeat – 1 minute. **Variant:** players are prohibited from playing one and two touches, excluding at the rebound	– goalkeepers should put the ball into play with kick or throw without a delay; – players should handle the ball quickly, and especially fast perform shot on goal while moving with the ball across the width of the pitch; – players should perform shots on goal from any, even inconvenient positions; – goalkeepers should move with sidesteps with bent legs without stepping too broadly or narrowly

Drill 2	
Drill description	**Technical tips**
One on one play with a «neutral» player acting for the team possessing the ball all the time, providing players' actions in the middle zone. Pitch size: 20 meters long, 12 meters wide. The middle zone 4 meters long is marked on the pitch 8 meters from the goal-line, and also the «goalkeepers' zones» no further than 3 meters from the goal-line. Players are acting in the middle zone all the time. Goalkeepers put the ball into play from the «goalkeeper's zone» to the middle zone of the pitch after catching it or when it has left the field through the goal-line or sidelines. Having received the ball in the middle zone, players from the attacking team try to shoot on goal from this zone with a **first touch.** Number of passes in the attack is **no more than two.** Play time in one repeat – 3 minutes	– goalkeepers should put the ball into play with kick or throw from the «goalkeepers zone» without a delay; – the player from the defending team should quickly attack the attacking player to whom the ball was sent, forcing him to act amid time and space shortage; – players should pass the ball to each other timely and precisely, providing the partner with time for performing a shot on goal; – players should perform shots on goal from any, even inconvenient positions; – goalkeepers should move with sidesteps with bent legs without stepping too broadly or narrowly

Drill 3	

Drill description	Technical tips
Two on two play with the «neutral» player acting all the time for the time possessing the ball. Pitch size: 16 meters long, 22 meters wide. The half-way line is marked. Goalkeepers put the ball into play to their half of the pitch after catching it or when it has left the field through the goal-line or sidelines. Having received the ball on their half, players from the attacking team try to shoot on goal from any area of the pitch. Players are prohibited from passing to goalkeepers. Corners are not awarded. Offsides are given. Goal scored with a first touch counts as two. Goal scored at the rebound counts as two. Play time in one repeat – 3 minute. **Variant:** players should perform the first shot of goal in every attack from their half	– goalkeepers should put the ball into play with kick or throw without a delay; – players should handle the ball quickly, and especially fast perform shot on goal while moving with the ball across the width of the pitch; – while passing across the width of the pitch players should use every opportunity for shooting on goal with a first touch; – players should try to use every opportunity to finish off the ball into the net; – goalkeepers should move with sidesteps with bent legs without stepping too broadly or narrowly; – goalkeepers has to be ready for possible sending the ball opposite to their movement to the moment when the player shoots on goal

Drill 4	
Drill description	**Technical tips**
Three on three play with two «neutral» players acting all the time for the team possessing the ball providing shooting on goal with a first touch. Pitch size: 30 meters wide, 20 meters long. Three zones are marked on the pitch: two lateral 6 meters wide each and the middle 18 meters wide. Goalkeepers put the ball into play to lateral zones after catching it or when it crosses the goal-line and sidelines. Shots on goal are performed obligingly from the **middle zone with a first touch** after a pass from the lateral zone. Number of passes in the attack is **no more than three.** Corners are not awarded. Offsides are not given. Goal scored at the rebound counts as two. Play time in one repeat – 5 minute. **Variant:** three on three play with the «neutral» player acting all the time for the time possessing the ball	– goalkeepers should put the ball into play with kick or throw without a delay; – any player may perform a pass from the lateral zone; – players should pass the ball as accurately as possible (at feet) for shooting on goal and use every opportunity for shooting on goal with a first touch; – players should try to use every opportunity to finish off the ball into the net; – goalkeepers should move with sidesteps with bent legs without stepping too broadly or narrowly; – goalkeepers has to be ready for possible sending the ball opposite to their movement to the moment when the player shoots on goal

Drill 5	
Drill description	**Technical tips**
Six attacking on two defending players play in two zones providing permanent actions of three attacking and one defending player in each zone and performing passes from zone to zone with a mounted trajectory. Two zones 18 meters wide and 12 meters long are marked on the pitch opposite to each other with a short sides at 10 meters. Goals are mounted on the opposite long sides of different zones. Three attacking and one defending player act in each zone all the time. Players are prohibited from moving from zone to zone. 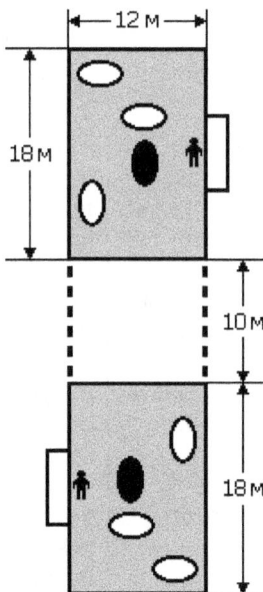	– goalkeepers should put the ball into play with kick or throw without a delay; – attacking players received the ball from the goalkeeper should pass the ball to each other timely and precisely, providing the partner with time for performing a pass into the opposite zone; – while passing into the opposite zone attacking players received the ball from the goalkeeper should consider the possibility of goalkeeper going out of the goal to intercept the ball; – attacking players received the ball from the goalkeeper may send the ball also into the net in case the goalkeeper takes obviously wrong position; – attacking players should act simultaneously while trying to deliver the ball from zone to zone;

92

Task 5 continuation

Goalkeepers put the ball into play to the zone where they protect their goal after catching it or when it leaves this area.	– having received the ball from the other zone, attacking players should quickly finish the attack with a shot on goal;
Attacking players try to pass the ball into the opposite zone to their partner with a mounted trajectory for shooting on goal.	
Number of passes to each other by attacking players received the ball from the goalkeeper before sending it to the opposite zone is **no more than two.**	– players should perform shots on goal from any, even inconvenient positions;
Number of passes to each other by attacking players received the ball from the opposite zone before shooting on goal is **no more than one.**	– defending players should try intercept the ball, quickly attack the attacking player to whom the ball was sent, forcing him to act amid time and space shortage;
Number of touches by each of attacking players received the ball from the opposite zone before shooting on goal is **no more than two.**	
One of defending players tries to prevent attacking players from passing into the opposite zone, while the another – to perform a shot on goal.	– goalkeepers should move with sidesteps with bent legs without stepping too broadly or narrowly;
The task for six attacking players is to score as much goals as possible in a definite time.	
Offsides are given in the moment of passing from one zone to another.	
Goal scored with a first touch counts as two.	– when a player performs a pass from zone to zone, goalkeepers should take such position that it would be possible to perform the interception of the ball among other things
Goal scored at the rebound counts as two.	
Variant: zones are marked diagonally to each other so that passes from zone to zone were performed diagonally relative to the goal-line	

Drills for training catching and blocking the ball by goalkeepers when caught wrong-footed in case of sudden change in trajectory of the ball flying into the net as a result of a touch by the player

Drill 1	
Drill description	**Technical tips**
Three on three play providing two players acting in the defensive zone and one in the attacking zone all the time. Pitch size: 12 meters wide, 22 meters long. Three zones are marked on the pitch: attacking and defensive 8 meters long each and the middle 6 meters long. In each team two players act in their team defensive zone, and one – in the attacking zone all the time. Players are prohibited from moving from zone to zone.	– goalkeepers should put the ball into play with kick or throw without a delay; – the player from the defending team acting in the attacking zone should quickly attack the player from the attacking team to whom the ball is passed, forcing him to act amid time and space shortage; – players should pass the ball to the partner timely and precisely, providing him with time for performing a shot on goal; – players should handle the ball quickly, and especially fast perform the strike motion while shooting on goal;

Task 1 continuation

Goalkeepers put the ball into play to their team defensive zone after catching it or when it crosses the goal-line and sidelines. Players from the attacking team, acting in the defensive zone, try to outplay one player from the defending zone and shoot from this zone **over the pitch surface.** Number of passes by players from the attacking team, acting in the defensive zone, is **no more than two.** Player from the attacking team, acting in the attacking zone, tries to reduce the visibility for the goalkeeper, change the direction of the ball to the goal and finish off the ball into the net. Player from the defending team, acting in the opponent's defensive zone, tries to tackle the ball and shoot on goal or pass to partners in his team defensive zone. Players from the defending team, acting in the defensive zone, try to block the ball moving into the net, prevent the opponent from shooting on goal or passing to partners in his team defensive zone. Corners are not awarded. Offsides are not given. Goal scored with a ricochet counts as two. Goal scored at the rebound counts as two. Play time in one repeat – 5 minute. **Variant:** goals are mounted at the corners of the pitch diagonally relative to each other	– players from the attacking team, acting both on the defensive and the attacking zones, should shoot on goal from any, even inconvenient positions; – player from the attacking team, acting in the attacking zone, should reduce the visibility for the goalkeeper to the greatest extent and try to change the direction of the ball, sent by the partner, to the goal; – player from the attacking team, acting in the attacking zone, should try to use every opportunity to finish off the ball into the net; – on course of actions on catching or blocking the ball sent by the player from the attacking team, acting in the defensive zone, goalkeepers should be ready for possible ball ricochet

Drill 2	
Drill description	**Technical tips**
Three on three play providing two players acting in the defensive zone and one in the attacking zone all the time, with two «neutral» players acting for the attacking team all the time. Pitch size: 12 meters wide, 26 meters long. Three zones are marked on the pitch: attacking and defensive 8 meters long each and the middle 10 meters long. In each team two players act in their team defensive zone, and one – in the attacking zone all the time. One «neutral» player acting in the defensive area, and another – in the attacking zone all the time. Players are prohibited from moving from zone to zone. 	– goalkeepers should put the ball into play with kick or throw without a delay; – the player from the defending team acting in the attacking zone should quickly attack the player from the attacking team to whom the ball is passed, forcing him to act amid time and space shortage; – players from the attacking team, acting in the defensive zone, should pass the ball to the partner timely and precisely, providing him with time for performing a shot on goal; – players should handle the ball quickly, and especially fast perform the strike motion while shooting on goal;

Task 2 continuation

Goalkeepers put the ball into play to their team defensive zone after catching it or when it crosses the goal-line and sidelines.

Players from the attacking team, acting in the defensive zone, try to outplay one player from the defending zone and shoot from this zone **over the pitch surface.**

Number of passes by players from the attacking team, acting in the defensive zone, is **no more than one.**

Players from the attacking team, acting in the attacking zone, try to reduce the visibility for the goalkeeper, change the direction of the ball to the goal and finish off the ball into the net.

Player from the defending team, acting in the opponent's defensive zone, tries to tackle the ball and shoot on goal or pass to partners in his team defensive zone.

Players from the defending team, acting in the defensive zone, try to block the ball moving into the net, prevent opponents from shooting on goal or passing to partners in his team defensive zone.

Corners are not awarded.

Offsides are not given.

Goal scored with a ricochet counts as two.

Goal scored at the rebound counts as two.

Play time in one repeat – 5 minute.

Variant: goals are mounted at the corners of the pitch diagonally relative to each other

– players from the attacking team, acting in the attacking zone, should reduce the visibility for the goalkeeper to the greatest extent and try to change the direction of the ball, sent by the partner, to the goal;

– players from the attacking team, acting in the attacking zone, should try to use every opportunity to finish off the ball into the net;

– players from the attacking team, acting both on the defensive and the attacking zones, should shoot on goal from any, even inconvenient positions;

– on course of actions on catching or blocking the ball sent by the player from the attacking team, acting in the defensive zone, goalkeepers should be ready for possible ball ricochet

Drill 3	
Drill description	**Technical tips**
One on one play with a «neutral» player acting for the team possessing the ball all the time, providing players' actions in the middle zone with two reserve goalkeepers acting for different teams. Pitch size: 40 meters long, 12 meters wide. The middle zone 6 meters long is marked on the pitch 17 meters from the goal-line, and also the «zone of reserve goalkeepers' actions» 2 meters long 7 meters from the goal-line. Players acting in the middle zone, while reserve goalkeepers – in «zones of reserve goalkeepers' actions».	– goalkeepers should put the ball into play with kick or throw without a delay without entering into the «zone of reserve goalkeepers' actions»; – the player from the defending team should quickly attack the attacking player to whom the ball was sent, forcing him to act amid time and space shortage; – players should handle the ball quickly, and especially fast perform the strike motion while shooting on goal; – players should pass the ball to each other timely and precisely, providing the partner with time for performing a shot on goal; – players may send the ball into the net over the pitch surface, with a rebound off the pitch surface and on air at different heights;

7 M

2 M

Zone of reserve goalkeeper's actions

8 M

6 M   Middle zone

8 M

Zone of reserve goalkeeper's actions

2 M

7 M

|← 12 M →|

Task 3 continuation

Goalkeepers put the ball into the middle zone of the pitch after catching it or when it has left the field through the goal-line or sidelines without entering into the «zone of reserve goalkeepers' actions». The reserve goalkeeper from the defending team doesn't prevent the ball from putting into play. Having received the ball in the middle zone, players from the attacking team try to outplay a player from the defending team and shoot on goal from this zone. Number of passes in the attack is **no more than two.** The reserve goalkeeper from the attacking team tries to reduce the visibility for the goalkeeper and change the direction of the ball into the net with any body part including hands, within the «zone of reserve goalkeepers' actions». Corners are not awarded. Goal scored with a ricochet counts as two. Play time in one repeat – 5 minute. **Variant:** two on two play with the «neutral» player acting for the team possessing the ball all the time, with two reserve goalkeepers acting for different teams providing that: – «neutral» player and one player from each team act in the middle zone all the time; – one player and the reserve goalkeeper from each team act in the «zone of reserve goalkeepers' actions» marked at the opponent's goal all the time; – player acting in the «zone of reserve goalkeepers' actions» may change the direction of the ball into the net with any body part except for hands	– players should perform shots on goal from any, even inconvenient positions; – players should use every opportunity for shooting on goal with a first touch; – reserve goalkeepers should reduce the visibility for goalkeepers to the greatest extent and try to change the direction of the ball, sent by the partner, to the goal; – goalkeepers should move with sidesteps with bent legs without stepping too broadly or narrowly; – on course of actions on catching or blocking the ball sent by the player from the attacking team goalkeepers should be ready for possible ball ricochet

Drill 4	
Drill description	**Technical tips**
Three on three play with two «neutral» players acting for the attacking team all the time, providing actions of two «neutral» players and two players from each team in the middle zone, one player from each team – at the «goalkeeper's zone» line. Pitch size: 12 meters wide, 25 meters long. Goalkeepers put the ball into play with a hand to the middle zone with a mounted trajectory after catching it or when it has left the field through the goal-line or sidelines. Players from the attacking team try to shoot on goal with a head from this zone at once or after a pass with a head to each other. Players are permitted to kick and pass the ball with a head after its rebound off the pitch surface. Player from the attacking team, acting at the line of «goalkeeper's zone», tries to reduce the visibility for the goalkeeper and change the direction of the ball to the goal with a head. Goal scored with a ricochet counts as two. Play time in one repeat – 5 minutes	– goalkeepers should put the ball into play without a delay so that a partner could perform a pass or a shot on goal with a head; – players should perform shots on goal with a head from any, even inconvenient positions; – players may put the ball into play with hands in cases when the ball touches the pitch surface; – players acting at the line of the «goalkeeper's zone» may change the direction of the ball into the net also in cases when it rebounds off the pitch surface; – on course of actions on catching and blocking the ball sent to the goal goalkeepers should be ready for possible ricochet

Drill 5	
Drill description	**Technical tips**
Five on five play with two «neutral» players acting for the attacking team all the time providing that the ball is put into play by goalkeepers on air with a high trajectory. Pitch size: 16 meters wide, 16 meters long. Goalkeepers put the ball into play with a kick «from hands» with a mounted trajectory after catching it or when it has left the field through the goal-line or sidelines for a partner to perform a pass with a head. Players from the attacking team try to shoot on goal with a foot or a head after a pass with a head or a rebound off the pitch surface. Number of passes in the attack by players from the attacking team is **no more than two.** Corners are not awarded. Offsides are not given. Goal scored with a ricochet counts as two. Goal scored at the rebound counts as two. Play time in one repeat – 5 minutes	– goalkeepers should put the ball into play without a delay so that a partner could perform a pass with a head; – players should handle the ball quickly, and especially fast perform the strike motion while shooting on goal; – players should perform shots on goal from any, even inconvenient positions; – players from the attacking team should try to change the direction of the ball into the goal; – on course of actions on catching and blocking the ball sent to the goal goalkeepers should be ready for possible ricochet

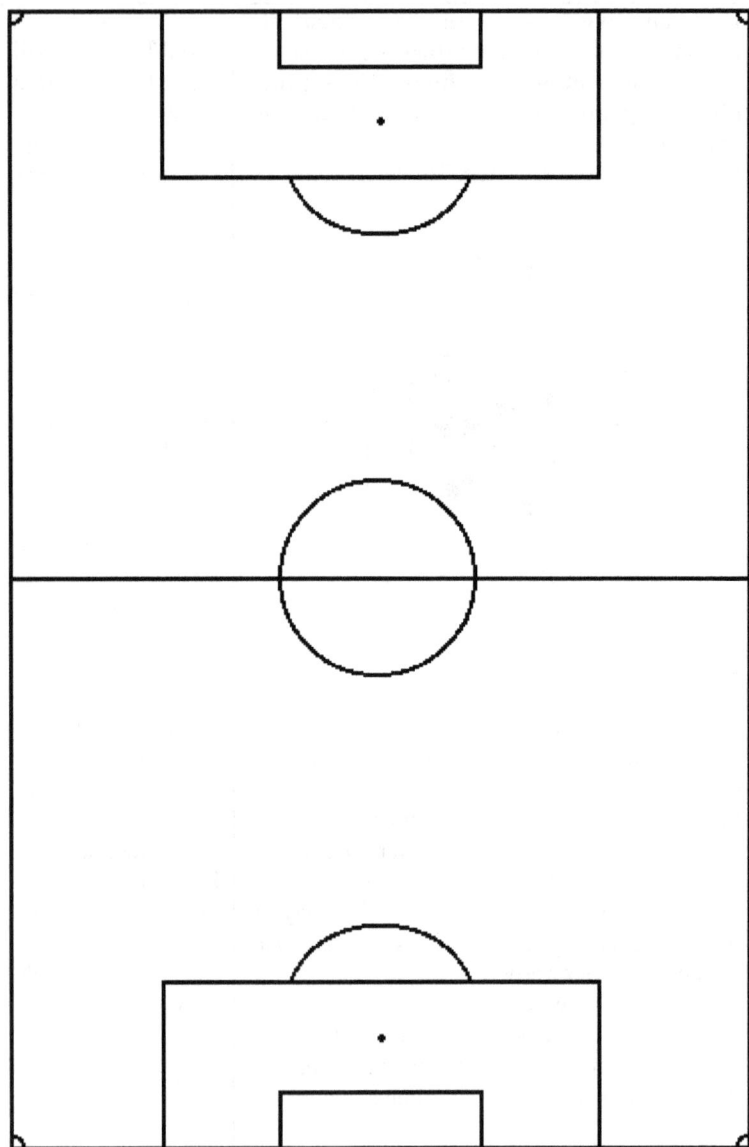

For notes

PART TWO
TRAINING CATCHING AND BLOCKING THE BALL IN TWO TEMPO

CHAPTER 7.
THE CONCEPT OF «GOALKEEPERS' PLAY IN TWO TEMPO»

There may occur situations in games while trying to score, when players from the attacking team, due to various reasons depending or non-depending on success of catching and blocking the ball by goalkeepers, get the second in a row opportunity to score after the rebound off the goalkeeper, players from the defending and attacking teams, goalposts and a bar.

For example, in matches of teams of high qualification (national teams) 10 per cent of goals at an average is scored exactly as a result of finishing off the ball into the net with a first touch (fig. 10).

Taking into the account that during the finishing off the ball into the net goals are scored not only with a first, but also with a second and a third touch, perfection of goalkeepers play prowess in these situations is one of the reserves of a team achieving higher results in competitions.

Volume of goals (as %)

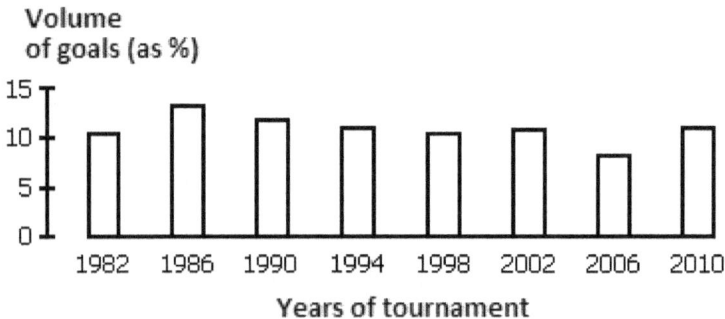

Fig. 10. Volume of goals (as a percentage of total) scored at World Cup in 1982-2010 while finishing off the ball into the net with a first touch

There are situations in games when the opponent has chances to score goal also after the second in a row attempt to catching or blocking the ball by the goalkeeper, but generally episodes of finishing play in football are concluded with a second in a row shot on goal anyhow.

The success of goalkeepers' actions while finishing off the ball into the net depends on ability to play in two tempo – perform the second in a row attempt to catch or block the ball without a delay, starting it from the position they got in after the first attempt to catch or block the ball.

The first and second in a row attempts to catch or block the ball may be performed by goalkeepers both in the same or in different directions (when caught wrong-footed).

It has to be noted that there are such situations in games when the ball reflected by the goalkeeper is still in the game, though there is no finishing off at all or it is exercised not immediately but after a while following a pass or movement of a player with the ball. In these cases goalkeepers also should be ready for finishing off the ball into the net, and so their second rate actions may present not only the second in a row attempt to catch or block the ball, but also taking of the best position for possible repeated performance of catching or blocking the ball.

Three fundamental components form the basis of goalkeepers play prowess in two tempo:

– the speed of performing of various second rate motive actions for catching and blocking the ball (getting up on feet, «shifting body», falling, jumping, starting speed-up);

– the ability to anticipate the moment, speed and direction of sending the ball on the player's movements and speed of oculogyric while tracking the ball;

– the mental willingness to perform the second in a row attempt to catch or block the ball, including with the risk of getting injured, immediately.

CHAPTER 8.
THE PROBLEM OF ORGANIZING OF TRAINING CATCHING AND BLOCKING THE BALL WHEN CAUGHT WRONG-FOOTED THE BALL IN TWO TEMPO

A large amount of attempts to perform catching and blocking the ball is necessary for perfecting of these actions by goalkeepers.

Though in practice the number of cases of catching and blocking the ball in two tempo in training of goalkeepers of youth and professional teams of different qualification is usually insignificant, as observations show.

If we consider drills used by in-field players for practicing scoring, when reasons why possibilities of finishing off the ball into the net occur infrequently consist in drills construction and specificity of players' actions while performing it.

There may be marked several characteristics in organizing of these drills that stipulate a small amount or even general lack of cases of finishing off the ball into the net by players.

First. In many drills players have to perform shots on goal from the outside of the 18-yard box. In these cases they generally just don't get in time to perform finishing off physically.

Second. Some drills are organized in such a manner that the possibility to finish off the ball into the net is excluded in principle. The following task may be hold up as an example of such drills organization.

Players should shoot on goal «in stream» from the outside of the 18-yard box or from the goal area, and, having shot, each one must immediately turn his back to the goal to receive the ball from the partner performing the task at his heels and pass the ball to him for shooting on goal (fig. 11).

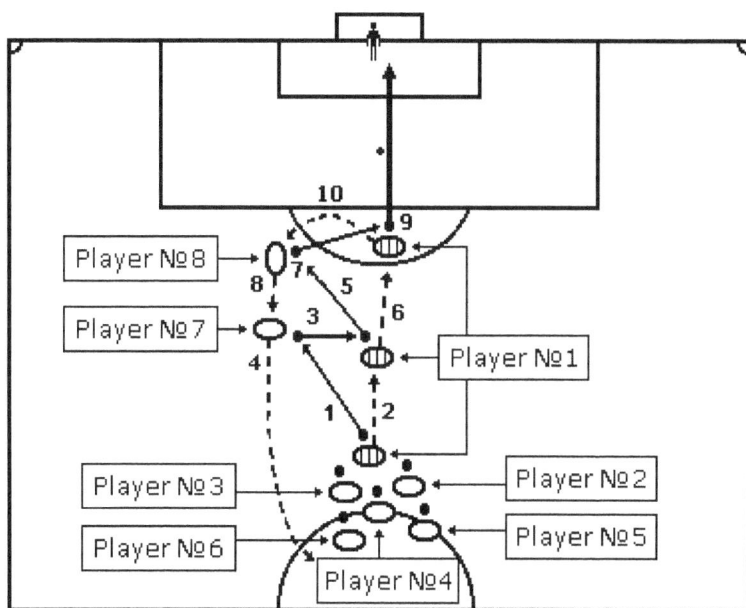

Fig. 11. Example of exercise for practicing shots on goal on course of which the possibility of finishing off the ball into the net is excluded, as player should immediately prepare to receive the ball from the partner after a shot

Third. Rare attempts to finish off the ball into the net on course of gaming drills are evidenced when such drills are performed in a considerable playing space with sufficiently high number of players in each team.

Concerning the goalkeepers' drills for training of catching and blocking the ball in two tempo it should be noted that more often than not it's performed in amount clearly deficient for improving this component of goalkeepers' play.

Therefore it may be acknowledged that successful goalkeepers' actions while playing in two tempo are very significant for the team, though generally it isn't trained systemically.

CHAPTER 9.
SPECIFICITY OF GOALKEEPERS' ACTIONS WHILE CATCHING AND BLOCKING THE BALL IN TWO TEMPO IN VARIOUS SITUATIONS

The specificity of goalkeepers' actions while catching and blocking the ball in two tempo in games is determined by several components:

– psychic determination to perform the second in a row attempt to catch or block the ball in any conditions without a delay;

– speed of actions while performing second attempts to catch or block the ball, which are generally necessary to begin from inconvenient positions;

– the ability to anticipate the moment and direction of sending the ball into the net on actions of a player performing a shot, because finishing off is generally performed from close and very close distance.

On course of developing methods of perfection of goalkeepers' play in two tempo it was necessary to define above all, from which positions they principally begin to perform the second in a row attempt to catch or block the ball while finishing off in games and in which situations, and also what do goalkeepers' second rate actions present specifically.

Observations on highly qualified goalkeepers' play have shown they may begin to perform the second in a row attempts of catching and blocking the ball while finishing off from various positions depending on point of a first shot on goal, speed, direction and trajectory of the ball.

More often second rate actions begin from following three positions:

– lying (reclining) on the back or sitting with arms leaning from the back face to the pitch;

     – lying on the side face to the pitch approx. perpendicularly to the direction of the ball sent into the net with a first shot, arms and legs bent to the body;

     – lying on the side face to the pitch approx. perpendicularly to the direction of the ball sent into the net with a first shot, arms and legs straighten (table. 2).

Table 2. Description of positions from which goalkeepers begin to perform the second attempt to catch or block the ball while finishing off most often (based on the results of observations on highly-qualified goalkeepers' actions)

Description of positions from which goalkeepers begin to perform second rate actions	In which play situations it may occur
Lying (reclining) on the back or sitting with arms leaning from the back face to the pitch	After attempts to reflect the ball flying at goalkeeper or very close to him with hands or feet
Lying on the side face to the pitch approx. perpendicularly to the direction of the ball sent into the net with a first shot, arms and legs bent to the body	After attempts to catch or block the ball flying not far from the goalkeeper with hands
Lying on the side face to the pitch approx. perpendicularly to the direction of the ball sent into the net with a first shot, arms and legs straighten	After attempts to catch or block the ball flying far away from the goalkeeper with hands

General kinds of goalkeepers' action while performing the second in a row attempt to catch or block the ball while finishing off are following:

First kind of actions. Return to the position «major goalkeeper stance», and then catching or blocking the ball in case the finishing off was performed by the opponent with some delay after the first shot.

Second kind of actions. Catching the ball bounced not far after the first attempt to catch or block the ball, or covering the direction of the ball after the second shot on goal in close vicinity to the player who performed a shot. These actions may be performed by goalkeepers both in the same direction the first attempt to catch or block the ball was performed in and in directions different from the direction of their action while performing the first attempt to catch or block the ball, i.e. when caught wrong-footed.

Third kind of actions. Catching or blocking the ball sent by the opponent with a second shot without a delay, performing these actions both in the same direction the first attempt to catch or block the ball was performed in and when caught wrong-footed.

It has to be noted that from the point of view of goalkeepers' psychology the goalkeepers' play in two tempo is similar to the play when caught wrong-footed during the ricochet: in both cases efficiency of actions largely depends on goalkeepers' motivation to perform second in a row attempt or movement for catching or blocking the ball.

In many cases catching and blocking the ball in two tempo by goalkeepers while finishing off are related to direct physical contact with the opponent and to sufficiently high risk of injury.

In this regard in psychology of goalkeepers' play in two tempo we may mark a distinctive component determined by the necessity for goalkeepers to ignore the risk of injury oftenly.

CHAPTER 10.
MAIN STRANDS OF WORK
WHILE TRAINING CATCHING
AND BLOCKING THE BALL
BY GOALKEEPERS IN TWO
TEMPO

Perfection of play in two tempo prowess by goalkeepers suggests two following main directions of work:

– performing special goalkeeper drills for training certain actions forming the basis of play in two tempo in different situations;

– training the play in two tempo as a whole in the context of drills for in-field players (normally beginning and gaming) which organization suggests possibility of players performing a large number of attempts to finish off the ball into the net.

In both cases certain methodological techniques allowing to improve efficiency of training work may be used while drill constructing.

It's problematically to bring about an improvement in prowess of goalkeepers' play in two tempo without a large number of these actions while training sessions. While looping second in a row attempts to catch or block the ball by goalkeepers during finishing off, often started from sitting or lying position, very high pressure is placed on their leg muscles, through the work of which the body generally moves through the space quickly.

Taking this into account, performance of additional work on development of strength capabilities of leg muscles may become necessary for certain goalkeepers on course of training catching and blocking the ball in two tempo.

CHAPTER 11.
SPECIAL EXERCISES
FOR TRAINING CATCHING
AND BLOCKING THE BALL
BY GOALKEEPERS IN TWO
TEMPO IN VARIOUS
SITUATIONS

11. 1. Organizing special exercises for training of catching and blocking the ball by goalkeepers in two tempo by goalkeepers

Taking into account second rate actions performed by goalkeepers while finishing off the ball into the net in games, and positions it starts from more often, three sets of special goalkeeper drills for perfection of play in two tempo in various situations.

Sets include three kinds of drills suggesting goalkeepers perform:

a) actions simulating second attempts of catching and blocking the ball while finishing off or catching and blocking static ball;

b) catching and blocking moving ball as a real second in a row attempt to catch or block the ball while finishing off;

c) two in a row attempts to catch and block the ball while sending two balls into the net with two shots.

Drills of the first kind are designed for raising the speed of goalkeepers' movements. Absence of moving ball in some of these drills as an impetus to display the maximum movement speed may be compensated by such drill organization when two neighbored goalkeepers perform the same drill competing in speed of its performance.

Quickness of movements largely depends on rational technique of its performance. Particularly, when goalkeepers have to begin catching and blocking the ball from the lying on the side position, they can quickly rise by means of sharp movements with shoulders and legs without leaning on elbows and knees.

In drills of the second kind goalkeepers catch the ball that seems to bounce not far from them after the reflection of the first shot on goal, and also catch or block the ball after shots presenting finishing off.

In these cases they are required to appreciate the position and motion of the ball or anticipate the moment and direction of sending the ball by a player on his actions, and also it is necessary to do on course of movements beginning from inconvenient position.

A shot presenting finishing off the ball into the net should be performed from close distance to train reactions of anticipation of the moment and direction of sending the ball on player's actions exactly, while the ball should be sent at a distance of actual reach of the goalkeeper.

While performing drills of the third kind goalkeepers must reflect two balls in a row without a delay. In this regard while organizing these drills it is necessary to turn attention to the following nuance.

For training of play in two tempo it is necessary for goalkeepers to reflect the ball after the first shot, though it is inappropriate to require them to reflect the ball after the first shot towards a partner precisely for him to perform the second shot immediately. This may result in developing a goalkeeper's habit to reflect the ball in front of himself, and so in deterioration of prowess in catching the ball after the first shot on goal.

Therefore two balls should be used in drills suggesting performance of two in a row attempts of catching or blocking the ball by goalkeepers, while shots on goal may be performed by one or two goalkeeper's partners.

Following are sets of special exercises for training catching and blocking the ball in two tempo by goalkeepers in different situations.

11. 2. Sets of special drills for training of catching and blocking the ball in two tempo by goalkeepers

Set 1
Drills for training catching and blocking the ball sent with a second shot after return to the position «major goalkeeper stance»

Drill № 1	
Drill description	**Technical tips**
The goalkeeper takes one of positions from which second attempts to catch or block the ball while finishing off commence more often: – lying (reclining) on the back or sitting with arms leaning from the back face to the pitch; – lying on he side face to the pitch, arms and legs bent to the body; – lying on the side face to the pitch, arms and legs straighten. The coach with the ball is positioned opposite to the goalkeeper 7 meters from him. The coach sends the ball with a foot over the pitch surface towards the goalkeeper, with a rebound off the pitch surface and above the goalkeeper at different heights with such speed that: – goalkeeper could catch the ball in the «major goalkeeper stance» position, beginning to get up on feet at the moment of shooting; – there is no pause between taking the «major goalkeeper stance» position and catching the ball by the goalkeeper. At the moment when the coach kicks the ball the goalkeeper begins to get up on feet quickly, takes the «major goalkeeper stance» position and catches the ball	– the coach should send the ball precisely towards the goalkeeper; – the goalkeeper should get into the «major goalkeeper stance» position at a maximum speed; – the coach should send the ball exactly with such speed that goalkeeper could catch the ball in «major goalkeeper stance» position, getting up on feet with a maximum speed; – while getting into the «major goalkeeper stance» position, the goalkeeper should track the ball all the time

114

Drill № 2	
Drill description	**Technical tips**
The goalkeeper takes one of positions from which second attempts to catch or block the ball while finishing off commence more often: – lying (reclining) on the back or sitting with arms leaning from the back face to the pitch; – lying on the side face to the pitch, arms and legs bent to the body; – lying on the side face to the pitch, arms and legs straighten. The coach with the ball is positioned opposite to the goalkeeper 7 meters from him. On a signal the goalkeeper quickly gets into the «major goalkeepcr stance» position. The coach immediately sends the ball with a foot aside from the goalkeeper at a distance of actual reach with different trajectories with a high speed. The goalkeeper catches or blocks the ball	– the goalkeeper should get into the «major goalkeeper stance» position at a maximum speed; – the coach should send the ball towards the goalkeeper with a necessary precision and speed at the moment when he gets into the «major goalkeeper stance» position

Drill № 3	
Drill description	**Technical tips**
The goalkeeper is positioned in the middle of the goal, the coach with two balls – opposite to the goalkeeper 7 meters from the goal-line. The coach sends the first ball with a foot aside from the goalkeeper with different trajectories and high speed so that the goalkeeper would catch or block the ball diving on the pitch. After catching or blocking the first ball the goalkeeper quickly gets into the «major goalkeeper stance» position. The coach immediately sends the second ball with a foot aside from the goalkeeper at a distance of actual reach with different trajectories with a high speed. The goalkeeper catches or blocks the second ball	– the goalkeeper should get into «major goalkeeper stance» position after catching or blocking the first ball at a maximum speed; – depending on the direction and speed of sending the second ball by the coach the goalkeeper may catch or block the ball second rate in supporting position, while diving and jumping

Set 2
Drills for training catching and blocking the ball near the goalkeeper after blocking the first shot

Drill № 1	
Drill description	**Technical tips**
The goalkeeper takes one of positions from which second attempts to catch or block the ball while finishing off commence more often: – lying (reclining) on the back or sitting with arms leaning from the back face to the pitch; – lying on the side face to the pitch, arms and legs bent to the body; – lying on the side face to the pitch, arms and legs straighten. The ball is set in front of the goalkeeper 3 meters from him. On a signal the goalkeeper quickly moves to the ball and catches (covers up) the static ball. **Variants:** a) points of setting the ball are varied relative to the goalkeeper (to the left, to the right and behind the goalkeeper); b) the coach with the ball is positioned near the goalkeeper and tosses the ball lowly above the pitch surface, while the goalkeeper on a signal catches the ball bouncing off the pitch surface; c) two goalkeepers, positioned close to each other, take one of positions from which second attempts of catching or blocking the ball while finishing off commence more often, and on a signal try to catch (cover up) the ball, set in front of each of them while diving, faster than the partner	– the goalkeeper should catch (cover up) the ball at a maximum speed; – the goalkeeper should move to the ball along the shortest trajectory; – the goalkeeper can catch (cover up) the ball while diving with advancing and while jumping forward or forward and to the side with diving on the pitch; – for exclusion the possibility of injury while catching (covering up) the ball while jumping forward or forward and to the side it is reasonably for the goalkeeper to land with certain sequence in touching the pitch with various parts of locomotion system (with calf, hip, pelvis, body and hands or underarms, with shoulder, body, pelvis and legs)

Drill № 2	
Drill description	**Technical tips**
A circle 5 meters in diameter is marked on the pitch. The goalkeeper is positioned at the center of the marked circle and takes one of positions from which second attempts to catch or block the ball while finishing off commence more often: – lying (reclining) on the back or sitting with arms leaning from the back face to the pitch; – lying on the side face to the pitch, arms and legs bent to the body; – lying on the side face to the pitch, arms and legs straightcn. The coach with the ball is positioned opposite to the goalkeeper 3 meters from him. The coach sends the ball with a hand in different repeats chaotically in different directions relative to the goalkeeper so that he could catch the ball in the marked circle, beginning to act at the moment of a throw. Balls are sent over the pitch surface, with a rebound off the pitch surface and on air at different heights: – towards the goalkeeper; – to the left and to the right side from the goalkeeper; – in front of the goalkeeper; – directly in front of the goalkeeper and into the area behind him. The goalkeeper moves to the ball and catches **moving** ball precluding it from getting beyond the marked circle. **Variants:** a) points of the coach's position are varied relative to the goalkeeper (to the left, to the right and behind the goalkeeper); b) the diameter of the marked circle is increased up to 7 meters	– the coach should send the ball with necessary precision and speed for the goalkeeper to catch the ball in the marked circle acting at a maximum speed; – depending on the direction and speed of sending thc ball by the coach into the marked circle the goalkeeper may catch the ball in supporting position, while diving and jumping; – for exclusion the possibility of injury while catching the ball while jumping forward, to the side, forward and to the side it is reasonably for the goalkeeper to land with certain sequence in touching the pitch with various parts of locomotion system (with calf, hip, pelvis, body and hands or underarms, with shoulder, body, pelvis and legs)

Drill № 3	
Drill description	**Technical tips**
The goalkeeper's partner with the ball is positioned opposite to the middle of the goal 13 meters from the goal-line, the coach with the ball – in the goal beyond the goal-line. The goalkeeper takes position in the goal for catching or blocking the ball in case the partner shoots on goal. The partner sends the ball into the net with a foot with different trajectories and high speed so that the goalkeeper would catch or block the ball diving on the pitch. In case the goalkeeper reflects the ball not far from him, he catches it quickly. In case the goalkeeper catches the ball or reflects it far away, the coach immediately sends his ball with a hand with different directions over the pitch surface, with a rebound off the pitch surface and on air at different heights so that the goalkeeper can catch the ball above 4-5 meters from him, acting at a maximum speed. The goalkeeper catches the second ball. **Variant:** points of the coach's position beyond the goal-line and the goalkeeper's partner across the width and along the length of the pitch	– the goalkeeper's partner should send the ball with necessary precision and speed for goalkeeper to catch or block the ball obligingly with diving on the pitch; – the goalkeeper should catch the ball, reflected after the partner's shot on goal, second rate at a maximum speed; – the coach should send the ball away from the goalkeeper with necessary precision and speed for him to catch the ball second rate no further than 4-5 meters from him, acting at a maximum speed; – the coach should vary direction and trajectory of sending the ball away from the goalkeeper in different task repeats chaotically

Set 3
Drills for training catching and blocking the ball sent with a second shot without a delay

Drill № 1	
Drill description	**Technical tips**
The goalkeeper is positioned in the middle of the goal and takes one of positions from which second attempts to catch or block the ball while finishing off commence more often: – lying (reclining) on the back or sitting with arms leaning from the back face to the pitch; – lying on the side face to the pitch, arms and legs bent to the body; – lying on the side face to the pitch, arms and legs straighten. The coach with the ball is positioned opposite to the middle of the goal 11 meters from the goal-line. The coach sends the ball with a foot in different repeats **chaotically** in different directions relative to the goalkeeper at a distance of actual reach so that he could catch or block the ball, beginning to act at the moment of a shot. Balls are sent over the pitch surface, with a rebound off the pitch surface and on air at different heights: – towards the goalkeeper; – to the left and to the right side from the goalkeeper; – above the goalkeeper. The goalkeeper catches or blocks the ball. **Variants:** a) points of the goalkeeper's position across the width of the pitch within the goal width and along the length of the pitch 3-4 meters from the goal-line; b) points of the coach's position are varied across the width and along the length of the pitch	– the coach should send the ball with necessary precision and speed for the goalkeeper to catch the ball acting at a maximum speed; – the goalkeeper should catch the ball at a maximum speed; – for exclusion the possibility of injury while catching and blocking the ball with diving it is reasonably for the goalkeeper to land with certain sequence in touching the pitch with various parts of locomotion system (with calf, hip, pelvis, body and hands or underarms, with shoulder, body, pelvis and legs)

Drill № 2	
Drill description	**Technical tips**
The coach with two balls is positioned opposite to the middle of the goal 13 meters from the goal-line, the goalkeeper takes position in the goal for catching and blocking the ball in case the coach shoots on goal. 13м The coach sends the ball into the net with a foot with different trajectories and high speed so that the goalkeeper would catch or block the ball diving on the pitch. In case the goalkeeper reflects the ball not far from him, he catches it quickly. In case the goalkeeper catches the ball or reflects it far away, the coach immediately sends the second ball into the net with a foot in different directions relative to the goalkeeper at a distance of actual reach. Balls are sent over the pitch surface, with a rebound off the pitch surface and on air at different heights: – towards the goalkeeper; – to the left and to the right side from the goalkeeper; – above the goalkeeper. The goalkeeper catches the second ball. **Variant:** points of the coach's position are varied across the width and along the length of the pitch	– the coach should send the first ball with necessary precision and speed for goalkeeper to catch or block the ball obligingly with diving on the pitch; – the goalkeeper should catch the ball, reflected after the coach's first shot on goal, second rate at a maximum speed; – the coach should send the second ball with necessary precision and speed for the goalkeeper to catch the ball second rate, acting at a maximum speed; – depending on the direction and speed of sending the second ball by the coach into the net the goalkeeper may catch the ball second rate in supporting position, while diving and jumping

Drill № 3	
Drill description	**Technical tips**
The goalkeeper's partner with the ball is positioned opposite to the middle of the goal 13 meters from the goal-line, the coach with the ball – opposite the goal area corner 7 meters from the goal-line. The goalkeeper takes position in the goal for catching or blocking the ball in case the partner shoots on goal. The partner sends the ball into the net with a foot with different trajectories and high speed so that the goalkeeper would catch or block the ball diving on the pitch. In case the goalkeeper reflects the ball not far from him, he catches it quickly. In case the goalkeeper catches the ball or reflects it far away, the coach immediately sends the ball into the net with a foot in different directions relative to the goalkeeper at a distance of actual reach. Balls are sent over the pitch surface, with a rebound off the pitch surface and on air at different heights: – to the left and to the right side from the goalkeeper; – above the goalkeeper. The goalkeeper catches the second ball. **Variant:** points of the goalkeeper's partners' and the coach's position are varied	– the goalkeeper's partner should send the ball with necessary precision and speed for goalkeeper to catch or block the ball obligingly with diving on the pitch; – the goalkeeper should catch the ball, reflected after the partner's shot on goal, second rate at a maximum speed; – the coach should send the ball with necessary precision and speed for the goalkeeper to catch the ball second rate, acting at a maximum speed; – the coach should vary direction and trajectory of sending the ball into the net in different task repeats chaotically

CHAPTER 12.
DRILLS FOR IN-FIELD PLAYERS SUGGESTING THE OPPORTUNITY OF TRAINING CATCHING AND BLOCKING THE BALL BY GOALKEEPERS IN TWO TEMPO

12. 1. Methods of increasing the number of goalkeepers' actions on catching and blocking the ball in two tempo in exercises on training of scoring goals by players

The necessary condition for perfection of play in two tempo by goalkeepers is a large amount of cases of finishing off the ball into the net by players.

The number of situations in which the finishing off is performed may be increased by making certain adjustments on organization of drills for training goalscoring. It refers equally both to drills with standard beginning of the attack and gaming drills.

Methods of increasing number of goalkeepers' actions on catching and blocking the ball in two tempo in normally beginning drills

We can use several methods for increasing number of finishings off the ball into the net while players perform normally beginning drills.

First. While players perform shots on goal in normally beginning drills, goalkeepers generally protect the goal alternately, changing each other at certain intervals of time.

Goalkeeper not involved in drill at a given point of time may be situated near the goal with the ball and after a player shoots on goal, depending on development of play situation, perform the natural finishing off into the net or simulate such actions in the following manner.

If the goalkeeper protecting the goal:

– reflects the ball towards him, he should shoot on goal with the same ball:

– lets the ball go not far from him, he should move to the ball forcing the goalkeeper to perform the second attempt to catch or block the ball at a maximum speed;

– catches the ball or reflects it to the side from the goal, he should occasionally and immediately shoot on goal with his ball, sending it in different direction relative to the goalkeeper at a distance of actual reach.

The goalkeeper who has been given a time for recovery may also be positioned with the ball behind the goal or near goalposts and pass it to the player who has just shot on goal imprecisely for him to perform the second in a row shot.

Second. Reflecting panels of a different height may be mounted at the goalposts beyond the goal-line. In this case some share of balls sent wide by players would bounce off the reflecting panels into the field and players could finish off these balls into the net.

Third. In certain cases for increasing number of goalkeepers' second rate actions it is possible to use if available such technical equipment as the boundary wall with the goal of a standard size marked on it. Drills for this purpose are organized in the following manner.

Players perform different shots on goal marked on the boundary wall and protected by goalkeepers, and while rebounding off the boundary wall they should obligingly shoot again, even if the goal was scored with a first shot.

Methods of increasing number of goalkeepers' actions on catching and blocking the ball in two tempo in gaming drills

In gaming drills the increased number of cases of finishing off may occur in case these drills are performed with the contiguous goals of a standard size in the small area of the pitch and little number of in-field players in teams.

This is due to the fact that in such conditions players may perform a high number of shots on goal from close and very close distance in a relatively short time, and so there may be quite a lot cases of finishing of the ball into the net.

For perfecting the second rate actions by goalkeepers there may be used many from those gaming drills with the contiguous goals which are recommended for training catching and blocking the ball when caught wrong-footed, especially during ricochets (see Chapter 6. «Drills for in-field player, suggesting the possibility of training catching and blocking the ball by goalkeepers when caught wrong-footed»).

The added incentive for increasing the number of play episodes of finishing off in gaming drills is the following encouraging of players: «a goal scored as a result of the finishing off counts as two or three».

Following are set of gaming drills with the contiguous goals for training catching and blocking the ball by goalkeepers in two tempo in different situations.

12. 2. Set of gaming drills with the contiguous goals for training of goal scoring by players with increased number of goalkeepers' actions on catching and blocking the ball in two tempo by goalkeepers

Drill № 1	
Drill description	**Technical tips**
Two on two play. Pitch size: 16 meters long, 18 meters wide. Goalkeepers put the ball into play after catching it or when it crosses the goal-line and sidelines. Players are permitted to pass the ball to goalkeepers only when putting it into play after fouls. Number of passes in the attack is **no more than two.** Corners are not awarded. Offsides are not given. Goal scored at the rebound counts as two. Play time in one repeat - 2 minute. **Variant:** two on two play with the «neutral» player acting all the time for the time possessing the ball	– players should handle the ball quickly, and especially fast perform a shot on goal; – players should perform shots on goal from any, even inconvenient positions; – players should try to use every opportunity to finish off the ball into the net; – with every shot on goal goalkeepers should be ready to perform the second in a row attempt to catch or block the ball without a delay; – goalkeepers should perform catching or blocking the ball second rate at a maximum speed

Drill № 2	
Drill description	**Technical tips**
Four on four play with a «neutral» player acting for the team possessing the ball all the time, providing actions of a «neutral» player and two players from each team in the middle zone, two players from each team – in the attacking zone. Pitch size: 25 meters long, 15 meters wide. Three zones are marked on the pitch: two zones of attack 7 meters long each and the middle 11 meters long. In each team two players act in the middle zone all the time, two are positioned on the sidelines of the pitch (one on the right, another on the left) in the attacking zone of their team. «Neutral» player is acting in the middle zone all the time. Players are prohibited from moving from zone to zone. 	– goalkeepers should put the ball into play with kick or throw without a delay; – players from the defending team should quickly attack the attacking player to whom the ball was sent, forcing him to act amid time and space shortage; – players should pass the ball to each other timely and precisely, providing the partner with time for performing a shot on goal; – players from the attacking team acting in the middle zone should handle the ball quickly, and especially fast perform a shot on goal; – players should perform shots on goal from any, even inconvenient positions; – players from the defending team should be ready for the opportunity to provide situations for finishing off;

126

Task № 2 continuation

Goalkeepers put the ball into the middle zone of the pitch after catching it or when it has left the field through the goal-line or sidelines without entering into the «zone of reserve goalkeepers' actions». Players from the attacking team acting in the middle zone try to outplay two players from the defending team and shoot on goal from this zone. Number of passes by players from the attacking team, acting in the middle zone, is **no more than three.** Players from the attacking team positioned on the sidelines in the attacking zone may move forward and backward and enter into this zone and finish off the ball into the net with a **first touch** when the goalkeeper reflects the ball into this zone. Players from the defending team acting in the middle zone try to tackle the ball and perform a shot on goal. One of players from the defending team acting in the middle zone may enter the attacking zone to get over the ball reflected by the goalkeeper after the opponent's shot on goal from the middle line. Corners are not awarded. Offsides are not given. Goal scored at the rebound counts as two. Play time in one repeat – 5 minute. **Variant:** players acting in the middle zone may pass the ball to partners positioned on the sidelines in the attacking zone who must return the ball to them with a first touch obligingly	– players from the attacking team positioned on the sidelines in the attacking zone, should try to use every opportunity to finish off the ball into the net; – players from the defending team should quickly decide on which of them would enter the opponents' attacking zone to prevent the finishing off; – goalkeepers should move with sidesteps with bent legs without stepping too broadly or narrowly; – with every shot on goal goalkeepers should be ready to perform the second in a row attempt to catch or block the ball without a delay; – goalkeepers should perform catching or blocking the ball second rate at a maximum speed

Drill № 3	

Drill description	Technical tips
Three on three play. Pitch size: 20 meters long, 20 meters wide. The half-way line is marked. 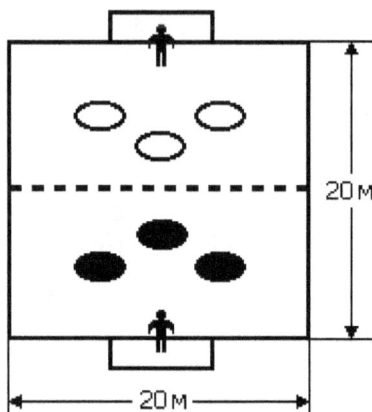 Goalkeepers put the ball into play after catching it or when it crosses the goal-line and sidelines. Players are prohibited from passing to goalkeepers. Number of passes in the attack is **no more than three.** Corners are not awarded. **Offsides are given.** Goal scored at the rebound counts as two. Play time in one repeat – 3 minute. **Variants:** a) goalkeepers put the ball into play in their half of the pitch, and in each attack players should perform the first shot on goal from their half; b) three on three play with the «neutral» player acting all the time for the team possessing the ball	– goalkeepers should put the ball into play with kick or throw without a delay; – players should handle the ball quickly, and especially fast perform a shot on goal; – players should perform shots on goal from any, even inconvenient positions; – players should try to use every opportunity to finish off the ball into the net; – goalkeepers should move with sidesteps with bent legs without stepping too broadly or narrowly; – with every shot on goal goalkeepers should be ready to perform the second in a row attempt to catch or block the ball without a delay

Drill № 4	
Drill description	**Technical tips**
Four on four play. Pitch size: 20 meters long, 25 meters wide. The half-way line is marked. Goalkeepers put the ball into play after catching it or when it crosses the goal-line and sidelines. Players are prohibited from passing to goalkeepers. Number of passes in the attack is **no more than four.** Corners are not awarded. **Offsides are given.** Goal scored at the rebound counts as two. Play time in one repeat – 5 minute. **Variants:** a) goalkeepers put the ball into play in their half of the pitch, and in each attack players should perform the first shot on goal from their half; b) four on four play with the «neutral» player acting all the time for the team possessing the ball	– goalkeepers should put the ball into play with kick or throw without a delay; – players should handle the ball quickly, and especially fast perform a shot on goal; – players should perform shots on goal from any, even inconvenient positions; – players should try to use every opportunity to finish off the ball into the net; – goalkeepers should move with sidesteps with bent legs without stepping too broadly or narrowly; – with every shot on goal goalkeepers should be ready to perform the second in a row attempt to catch or block the ball without a delay

Drill № 5	
Drill description	**Technical tips**
Four on four play with two «neutral» players acting for the attacking team all the time providing that the ball is put into play by goalkeepers on air with a high trajectory. Pitch size: 16 meters wide, 16 meters long. 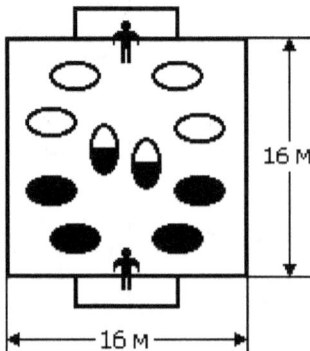 Goalkeepers put the ball into play with a kick «from hands» with a mounted trajectory after catching it or when it has left the field through the goal-line or sidelines for a partner to perform a pass with a head. Players from the attacking team try to shoot on goal with a foot or a head after a pass with a head or a rebound off the pitch surface. Number of passes in the attack by players from the attacking team is **no more than two.** Corners are not awarded. Offsides are not given. Goal scored at the rebound counts as two. Goal scored with a ricochet counts as two. Play time in one repeat – 5 minutes	– goalkeepers should put the ball into play without a delay so that a partner could perform a pass with a head; – players should handle the ball quickly, and especially fast perform a shot on goal; – players should perform shots on goal from any, even inconvenient positions; – players should try to use every opportunity to finish off the ball into the net; – goalkeepers should move with sidesteps with bent legs without stepping too broadly or narrowly; – with every shot on goal goalkeepers should be ready to perform the second in a row attempt to catch or block the ball without a delay

For notes

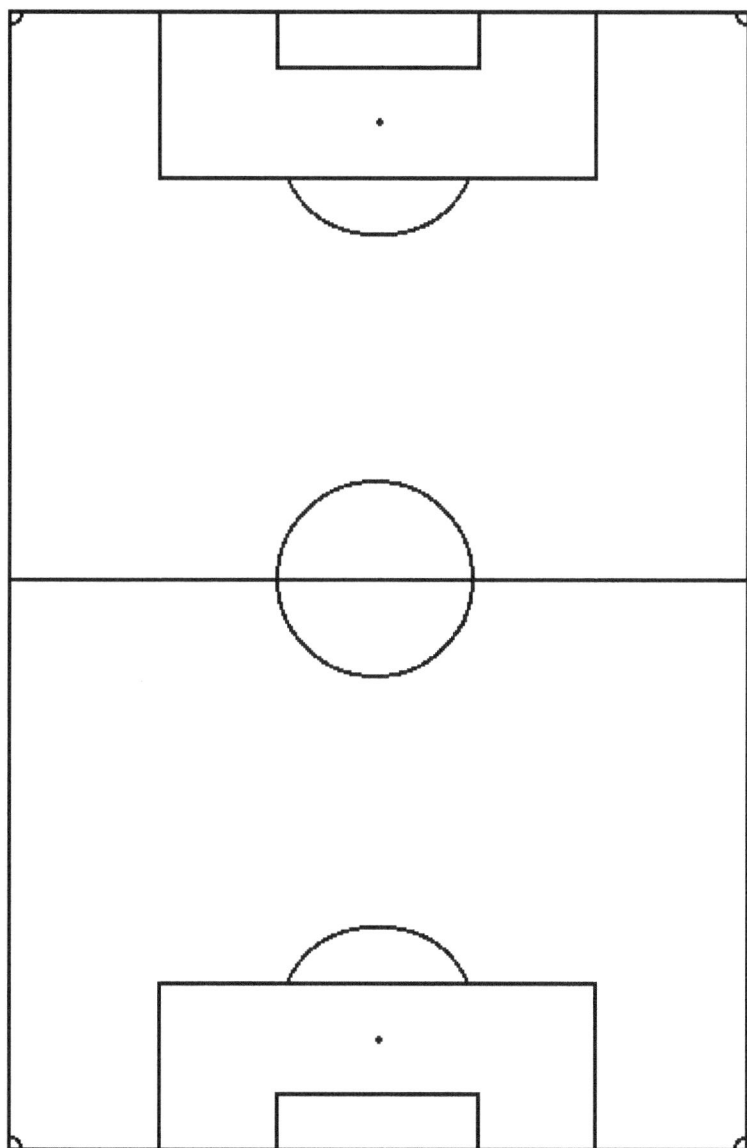

AFTERWORD

First. Play when caught wrong-footed presents a special kind of structure of goalkeepers' complex actions on protecting the goal. It is related to catching and blocking the ball sent opposite relative to the direction of goalkeeper's movement before the moment of shooting and applied in cases when the ball's trajectory suddenly changes on course of its flight towards the goal as a result of a touch by the player.

Since most of goals in games is conceded by goalkeepers exactly in situations when they have to play when caught wrong-footed, it is important to emphasize on training all actions occurring when caught wrong-footed.

Perfection of catching and blocking the ball by experienced goalkeepers when caught wrong-footed suggests two main strands of work:

– training of certain actions occurring while playing when caught wrong-footed in different situations using specially organized goalkeeper drills;

– training of play when caught wrong-footed in whole in the context of those team exercises in which situations of catching and blocking the ball by goalkeepers when caught wrong-footed in games may be simulated.

Taking into account the specificity of goalkeepers' actions while catching and blocking the ball when caught wrong-footed in games it is necessary to thoroughly explore play when caught wrong-footed in special goalkeeper exercises in situations when:

– goalkeepers move in one or another direction to take position for catching or blocking the ball before the moment when it is sent towards the goal;

– on course of flight towards the goal the ball suddenly changes its trajectory as a result of a touch by the player situated on its way.

Possibilities of perfecting catching and blocking the ball when caught wrong-footed by goalkeepers in drills performed by in-field players are due to how the attack finishing (goalscoring) is going on.

More efficient are those exercises which conditions suggest the uncertainty of time and place of shooting on goal by players and who would perform it, i.e. variativelly finishing drills. Class of drills presenting various variants of football game with the contiguous goals especially stands out among them.

Second. While performing shots on goal, passing and outplaying there may occur situations when it is necessary for goalkeepers to perform the second attempt to catch or block the ball without a delay, i.e. play in two tempo.

Since the success of goalkeepers' second rate actions while catching and blocking the ball largely determines the outcome of games, it is necessary to intentionally take measures to perfection of prowess of play in two tempo by them.

The specificity of goalkeepers' actions while catching and blocking the ball in two tempo is determined by several components:

– psychic determination to perform the second in a row attempt to catch or block the ball in any conditions without a delay;

– speed of actions while performing second attempts to catch or block the ball, which are generally necessary to begin from inconvenient positions;

– the ability to anticipate the moment and direction of sending the ball into the net on actions of a player performing a shot.

Perfection of play in two tempo prowess by goalkeepers suggests two main directions of work:

– performing special goalkeeper drills for training certain actions forming the basis of play in two tempo in different situations;

– training the play in two tempo as a whole in the context of drills for in-field players (normally beginning and gaming) which organization suggests possibility of a large number of attempts to finish off the ball into the net.

BIBLIOGRAPHY

Акимов А. Игра футбольного вратаря / А. Акимов. – М.: Физкультура и спорт, 1978. – 95 с.

Голомазов С., Чирва Б. Футбол. Тренировка вратаря / С. Голомазов, Б. Чирва. – М., РГАФК, 1996. – 200 с.

Голомазов С., Чирва Б. Футбол. Факторы, влияющие на успешность ловли и отражения мячей вратарями: метод. пособие. Выпуск 21 / С. Голомазов, Б. Чирва. – М., РГУФК, 2004. – 44 с.

Голомазов С., Чирва Б. Футбол. Методика тренировки вратарями ловли и отражения мячей «на два темпа»: метод. разработки для тренеров. Выпуск 25 / С. Голомазов, Б. Чирва. – М., РГУФК, 2005. – 24 с.

Голомазов С., Чирва Б. Футбол. Структура двигательной и психомоторной деятельности вратарей в игре: метод. пособие. Выпуск 26 / С. Голомазов, Б. Чирва. – М., РГУФК, 2005. – 24 с.

Голомазов С., Чирва Б. Футбол. Факторы, обуславливающие мобилизационную готовность вратарей в игре: метод. пособие. Выпуск 27 / С. Голомазов, Б. Чирва. – М., РГУФК, 2005. – 44 с.

Голомазов С., Чирва Б. Футбол. Технические приемы игры вратарей: метод. пособие. Выпуск 29 / С. Голомазов, Б. Чирва. – М., РГУФК, 2006. – 39 с.

Голомазов С.В., Чирва Б.Г. Футбол. Теоретические основы тренировки ловли и отражения мячей вратарями / С.В. Голомазов, Б.Г. Чирва. – М.: ТВТ Дивизион, 2006. – 144 с.

Голомазов С.В., Чирва Б.Г. Футбол. Тренировка вратарями ловли и отражения мячей «на противоходе» и «на два темпа» / С.В. Голомазов, Б.Г. Чирва. – М.: ТВТ Дивизион, 2008. – 96 с.

Горский Л. Игра хоккейного вратаря / Л. Горский. – М.: Физкультура и спорт, 1974. – 142 с.

Гранаткин В., Фокин Е. Игра вратаря / В. Гранаткин, Е. Фокин. – 2-е изд. – М.: Физкультура и спорт, 1953. – 115 с.

Костелис Д. Отработка техники игры руками, ногами, отражения мячей, пробиваемых в угол ворот / Д. Костелис // «Футбол-Профи». – Донецк (Украина). – 2006. – № 2 (3). – С. 32-33.

Михайлов М. Особенности игры вратарей на выходах / М. Михайлов // «Футбол-Профи». – Донецк (Украина). – 2006. – № 1 (2). – С. 32-35.

Соломонко В.В. Как передвигаться вратарю / В.В. Соломонко // Спортивные игры. – 1968. – № 9. – С. 20.

Соломонко В.В. Тренировка вратаря в футболе / В.В. Соломонко. – Киев: Здоров'я, 1986. – 124 с.

Сурков Е. Антиципация в спорте / Е. Сурков Е. – М.: Физкультура и спорт, 1982. – 143 с.

Уроки Питера Шилтона // Еженедельник «Футбол». – 1997. – № 26. – С. 28.

Фокин Е. Игра вратаря / Е. Фокин. – М.: Физкультура и спорт, 1967. – 85 с.

Чанади А. Тренировка вратаря / А. Чанади // В книге: Футбол. Тренировка. – М.: Физкультура и спорт, 1985. – С. 240-256.

Чирва Б., Голомазов С. Футбол. Методика тренировки вратарями ловли и отражения мячей «на противоходе»: метод. разработки для тренеров. Выпуск 30 / Б. Чирва, С. Голомазов. – М., РГУФК, 2007. – 59 с.

Чирва Б.Г. Футбол. Игровые упражнения при сближенных воротах для тренировки техники игры / Б.Г. Чирва. – М.: ТВТ Дивизион, 2008. – 120 с.

Чирва Б.Г. Футбол. Первенство Европы 2008 г.: удары по воротам: метод. разработки для тренеров. Выпуск 31 / Б.Г. Чирва. – М., РГУФКСиТ, 2009. – 56 с.

Шамардин А.И. Исследование игровой деятельности вратарей в футболе и экспериментальное обоснование методики их подготовки: автореф. дис. ... канд. пед. наук / А.И. Шамардин; ГЦОЛИФК. – М., 1979. – 15 с.

ENCLOSURE

Points of finishing off with a foot with a first touch on Euro 2012 (according to observation on 31 matches)

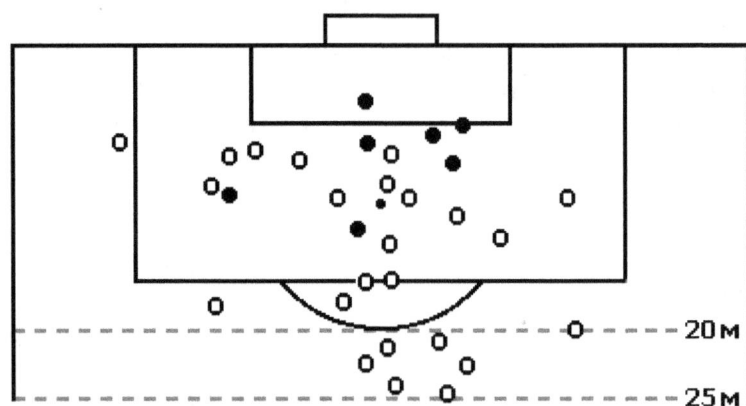

● Points of shooting resulted in goal
O Points of shooting not resulted in goal

Points of finishing off with a head on Euro 2012 (according to observation on 31 matches)

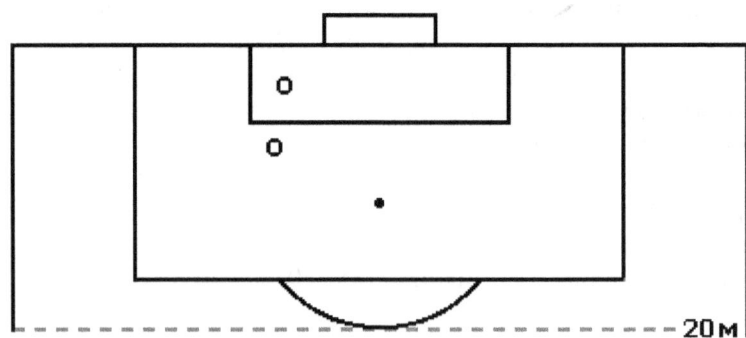

O Points of shooting not resulted in goal

www.ingramcontent.com/pod-product-compliance
Lightning Source LLC
Chambersburg PA
CBHW070114070426
42448CB00039B/2801